D0469851

quick meal solutions

MORE THAN 150 NEW, EASY, TASTY, AND NUTRITIOUS RECIPES FOR FAMILIES ON THE GO

Sandra K. Nissenberg, M.S., R.D.
Margaret L. Bogle, Ph.D., R.D.
Audrey C. Wright, M.S.

BICENTENNIAL
1807
WILEY
2007
BICENTENNIAL

John Wiley & Sons, Inc.

Published by John Wiley & Sons, Inc., Hoboken, New Jersey
Published simultaneously in Canada

Design and production by Navta Associates, Inc.

The information contained in this book is not intended to serve as a replacement for professional medical advice. Any use of the information in this book is at the reader's discretion. The author and the publisher specifically disclaim any and all liability arising directly or indirectly from the use or application of any information contained in this book. A health care professional should be consulted regarding your specific situation.

For general information about our other products and services, please contact our Customer Care Department within the United States at (800) 762-2974, outside the United States at (317) 572-3993 or fax (317) 572-4002.

Wiley also publishes its books in a variety of electronic formats. Some content that appears in print may not be available in electronic books. For more information about Wiley products, visit our web site at www.wiley.com.

Library of Congress Cataloging-in-Publication Data:

Nissenberg, Sandra K.
  Quick meal solutions : more than 150 new, easy, tasty, and nutritious recipes for families on the go / Sandra K. Nissenberg, Margaret L. Bogle, Audrey C. Wright.
    p. cm.
  Includes index.
    ISBN 978-0-471-75266-0 (paper)
  1. Quick and easy cookery. I. Bogle, Margaret L. II. Wright, Audrey C. III. Title.
  TX833.5.N57 2007
  641.5'55—dc22

                                                              2006016187

Printed in the United States of America

10 9 8 7 6 5 4 3 2 1

Contents

Acknowledgments

Special thanks to my husband, Andy, and my children, Heather and Corey, for allowing me weekend access to the computer and for offering to help with taste-testing recipes. Also, a special thanks to my great coauthors for meeting my demanding deadlines.

Sandy Nissenberg

Thanks go to all of the children and families with whom I have been privileged to interact over the years. Also, special thanks to my six grandchildren for their critiques of our recipes and nutrition advice and for being honest, as only children can be. And to my husband, Bill, who has supported me in whatever endeavors I have pursued, and for his editorial reading.

Margaret Bogle

I want to thank my family and friends, who were always willing to try my recipes and give me honest reviews. Also, thanks to my precious grandchildren, who thought that whatever I prepared was special.

Audrey Wright

Introduction

Since we first brought you our *Quick Meals for Healthy Kids and Busy Parents* in 1995, we have found that lifestyles have gotten even busier than they were ten years ago. Families are still finding little time to plan meals, organize recipes and shopping lists, and take the necessary time to put together a family meal. Parents are still looking for that magic answer to how they can get their families fed quickly and healthfully.

We have seen trends in cooking and recipe development moving toward those quick and easy foods, meals with four or fewer ingredients, one-dish meals, and meals that take no longer than twenty to thirty minutes to prepare. Common goals of many busy families are to get their families to eat right, choose nutritious foods, and of course, sit down for meals together. Of course, these are quite the ambitious goals, particularly when both parents work, kids run to after-school practices, and no one in the household seems to follow the same schedule.

That's why we are offering you our new book, *Quick Meal Solutions*. As registered dietitians and nutrition experts, we know it's not just about the recipes, but about the planning and organizing that puts meals on the table. We can collect all the "easy" recipes we want, but if we cannot find the time to keep necessary staples on hand, make grocery lists, or plan meals, we are getting no further toward accomplishing our goals.

So this new book is here to offer you all the above. We hope *Quick Meal Solutions* will accomplish the following:

- Help you understand how you and your family should eat. We're including a discussion of the new 2005 Dietary Guidelines for Americans and MyPyramid.

- Give you the tools you need to begin the planning process when it comes to keeping staples in the home, making shopping lists that work, understanding your grocery store, and planning ahead.

- Supply you with menu ideas that you can use or adapt to fit your family's needs and desires.

- Offer a collection of new, quick, and easy recipes that not only will satisfy and nourish your family but offer favorites that you can come back to time and again.

- Share our favorite "Quick Bites" of food and nutrition knowledge.

- Provide direction on preparing foods at home that can easily be taken on the road when time is not in your favor.

As we look ahead into the future, we see that there will be new approaches to convenience foods as fast and busy lifestyles continue. What we want to see are changes in how we manage our lifestyles to combat these trends. We hope you benefit from all the information we have included to help you get your busy life on the right track. You have nothing to lose and everything to gain. Why not give your family a new start toward a healthier and happier life?

1

What's Happening to Our Eating Habits Today?

Ready-to-eat, microwavable, drive-through, take-out, grab-and-go meals; desktop and dashboard dining; backseat breakfasts; eating out; one-dish meals: it's all about getting ourselves and our families fed as rapidly and healthfully as possible.

Everyone is in a hurry today. Time is at a premium. Two-parent working families are the norm rather than the exception. Kids are overscheduled with activities. As a result of all the busyness, cooking and eating at home have become less of a priority for many families. Yet maintaining the family unit—another priority—can be accomplished with a little planning. Our goal is to give you some suggestions, tools, and recipes to help with this important aspect of keeping a healthy family together.

Just forty or fifty years ago, women took charge of the cooking responsibilities in most households. Many women did not work outside the home, and they devoted much of their time to planning, shopping, and feeding their families. It was not uncommon for meals to take three to five hours each day on average to prepare. Families convened at regular dinner hours, ate together, shared stories about their days, enjoyed one another's company, and even helped to clean up! On top of all this, there were no microwave ovens, toaster ovens, convenience meals, or prepackaged one-dish dinners.

Over the years, much has changed—women have entered the workplace in record numbers; many children spend their days in day care, engaged in extracurricular activities, or on the run; commuting times have increased dramatically, adding extra hours to the already long workday; and less and less effort is put into resolving that old familiar question, "What's for dinner tonight?"

Food manufacturers have tried to help by addressing the concerns of busy households. Grocery stores and supermarkets have followed suit. Food selections at the grocery store have changed dramatically over the years to help meet today's trends and needs. Fast-food establishments have stepped up to offer convenience meals, too.

Consumers are aware of the importance of good nutrition, but often need to take a more active role in meeting their daily requirements. Families continue to be interested in convenience foods but should also learn how these foods play into their future health and wellness.

Current Food Trends

Let's look at some of the trends we see today. Food trends are big business. Think of all the trends that have popped up in recent years. Buzzwords in the food industry can make or break many food products. The media hit on a topic and everyone wants to jump on the bandwagon, sometimes making it difficult for us to choose what is right for our families. Do you remember when "oat bran" was a major topic of discussion and everyone was buying oats galore? Or when organics first hit the market? How about the "low-fat" craze? We're sure you are familiar with the "low-carb" trend. Have you heard of "slow foods"? What could possibly be next? As we move ahead to the coming years, here's a list of predictions and trends:

- The use of low-carb foods and low-carb diets is on the decline.
- Trans fats will disappear from foods; there will be more discussion about removing hydrogenated fats from existing foods as noted on food labels.
- Whole grains and high fiber will be popular in the next few years.

- More sugar substitutes will hit the market.
- More emphasis will be placed on kids' nutrition. Everyone is doing it; there are kids' cooking classes, kids' cookbooks, and kids' cooking programs on TV.
- More fathers will care for children as stay-at-home dads will be a prime target for food marketers.
- Ethnic options are growing, with more variety and less fat.
- Grocery shopping is changing. More people are shopping online, others via cell phones and personal digital assistants. Smart grocery carts will show up, too.
- Supercenters and warehouse stores are popping up everywhere. Buy it all in one extra-large location and in extra-large packages.
- Supermarket checkers are becoming outmoded. More self-checkouts are being built at grocery stores across the United States. This offers shoppers another avenue to save time and make grocery shopping a faster experience overall.
- More families are eating out than ever before.
- More fresh fruits and vegetables, including ethnic produce, will be available at smaller stores.
- Children will have money to spend on fast food and convenience stores.
- Families will spend more time in leisure and recreational activities.

Eating at Home and Away

Does anyone cook at home anymore? The term *home cooking* doesn't mean the same thing that it did in the days when our grandmothers grew up. Back then, meal preparation was an all-day affair. All the women and the girls in the household pitched in to help. Young women had to learn their way around a kitchen, how to plan a meal, how to use various appliances, how to set the table, and how to serve their families hearty meals. Today, this is no longer the case. There is at least one generation of kids who have little or no experience with home cooking. Kids also know little about setting the table or even table manners.

Today, when people do cook at home, they often take advantage of the many time-saving foods available—boneless, skinless chicken breasts and fish fillets; prepared stuffing, rice dishes, and noodles; pasta sauces; refrigerated breads and rolls; and many, many more. There's nothing wrong with taking shortcuts as long as they work for you and will provide for your family's nutritional needs. In fact, shortcuts can be the secret to feeding your family quickly and healthfully. What's interesting is that even with all these shortcuts, there are still many people who can't find the time or the desire to cook and eat at home.

Eating Out

Public dining dates back to the 1700s and likely began in France. Historians indicate that the first cafeteria opened in the United States in the 1800s. The concept of drive-ins and fast food started sometime before World War II, its popularity taking off with the creation of McDonald's in the 1950s.

Dining out became a social diversion. Specialty restaurants offering specific types of food, like seafood or Italian, soon followed. Restaurants have since become lavish in decor, food preparation, and services, as well as casual for families and fast for quick eating. Modern restaurants also offer informal service and atmosphere with a wide range of food selections. Restaurants are now found everywhere, offering every type of food and catering to every budget. No wonder eating out has become so popular over the years.

The Convenience Food Movement

As early as the 1950s, when many women were going into the workforce and household chores sometimes took a backseat to other activities, the Swanson brothers dreamed up the idea of creating complete frozen meals in individual servings that could easily be reheated and enjoyed in place of home-cooked meals. Some people referred to these meals as TV dinners because advertisements showed them being eaten in front of a newly popular invention—the television set. One example of early frozen TV dinners consisted of preportioned turkey slices, stuffing with gravy, sweet potatoes, and peas on an aluminum dish that could easily be reheated in the oven and carried on a tray into the living room. This may have started the trend toward frozen and convenience meals. Frozen TV dinners have come a long way since then, with so many different options now available. Some of them even meet the requirements of various special diets. Have you ever taken a moment to look at all the frozen meals in your supermarket? The convenience food industry has expanded to a whole new level. There are frozen low-calorie diet meals, side dishes, kid-friendly foods, pastas, stir-fries, and so much more. Obviously, nothing can beat that down-home taste of homemade, but alternatives are sure a plus.

Knowing the concerns about getting balanced, healthful foods on the table that families face today, manufacturers continually come to the rescue with options that may or may not be the best solution for your family. Not all are frozen, not all are complete meals. Many manufacturers try to help cooks feel as if they are still putting a meal together—semi-homemade or speed-scratch, as it's often called. Long gone are the days for many when it comes to completely homemade. Here are some of the alternatives available today (and more will likely hit the marketplace in the future).

Ready-to-Eat Foods and Home Meal Replacements

Often, dinnertime approaches before anyone realizes there's nothing to eat or prepare at home. That's when ready-to-eat foods or home meal replacements may come in handy. Fully prepared meals like fast-food fare, Chinese or pizza delivery services, local

QUICK BITE

Make your takeout a meal: Bring home chicken wings—add cole slaw and fresh fruit. Bring home lasagna—add a tossed salad and canned fruit. Bring home hamburgers—add baby carrots and fresh pepper slices—and you're done.

restaurant carry-outs, meal deals at the local supermarket—all of these are ready-to-eat foods. Bring the food home, lay it out on the table, and serve it to the family. In some ways, it takes away from the idea of a homemade dinner, but these meals can serve busy families in a pinch, and they can be both balanced and nutritious. Bringing the family together is key; the foods should be secondary. Offering a variety of food choices is also important, rather than focusing on who prepared them. Add a fresh tossed salad or some fruit, and your meal is complete. There is no end in sight to the trend of relying on ready-to-eat foods, so restaurants, groceries, and manufacturers are catering to this need.

Heat-and-Eat Foods

Getting the taste of homemade without the hassle is the advantage of certain ready-to-eat heat-and-eat foods. These meals are quick and easy to prepare; they give moms (and dads) a feeling of satisfaction with what they have accomplished; and they are often tasty, fresh, and nutritious. Fully cooked meats, like beef, turkey, and ribs, dressed in sauces and gravy, are heated in as few as five minutes in the microwave. They can be on the table with a side dish or two in no time. The cost of these meals is reasonable and will continue to be if manufacturers want families to keep purchasing them.

QUICK BITE

Keep bags of salad greens and prepared cole slaw mixes available for a quick side dish.

Custom Quick-Prep Meals

Many packaged meals allow consumers to customize meals to their own preferences. By adding your choice of chicken, beef, or shrimp to a prepackaged stir-fry, the meal becomes almost homemade. Then serve it with either rice, couscous, or pasta and, again, you have made a change to please your family.

Portable Meals

Take it with you. Phrases like *dashboard dining*, *desktop dining*, and *backseat breakfasts* have become new slang terms in the last few years. Eating in the car with the dashboard as your table or eating at your desk in the workplace is on the rise. Kids are now targeted as "backseat diners." Food manufacturers have noticed this trend and are creating packaged foods to meet these needs— foods that are easy to open as well as to consume. Beverage cup holders in cars can hold smoothies, snacks, and even quick hot foods like soup. Now it's possible to eat anywhere and every- where. Even nutritious breakfast bars, power bars, and fruit or granola bars can provide an energy boost in a few bites, but these snacks do not replace a meal. They may add some supplemental nutrition when you're on the run, but they're not the solution to maintaining a healthful diet.

These trends are not all bad. In fact, many of them offer excellent options and alternatives for today's lifestyles. It would be difficult not to take advantage of them, but they shouldn't replace every meal or substitute for the opportunity to sit down to dinner with your family. Our goal is to help you determine how these time-saving trends can work for you and your family. There will be certain times when portability, eating on the run, or con- venience foods may be the way to go.

In the pages ahead, you can balance these quick dinner solu- tions with meals that you plan, thus incorporating more meals at home into your busy schedule while still eating healthfully.

QUICK BITE

Set your dinner goals for the week according to your schedule.

Monday: Homemade spaghetti and meatballs, salad, garlic bread

Tuesday: Takeout at home, plus a salad

Wednesday: Leftover meatballs served on hoagie buns, plus cole slaw

Thursday: Frozen chicken cutlets, green beans, baked potatoes, fresh fruit

Friday: Quick beef stir-fry, rice, mandarin oranges

None of these meals takes more than thirty minutes to prepare.

2

Understanding and Using the 2005 Dietary Guidelines for Americans

M ost people want a measuring stick to help determine whether they are in fact eating healthful food and appropriate amounts to maintain a healthful lifestyle. The 2005 Dietary Guidelines for Americans provide just that—the best nutritional advice and the scientific basis for making healthful food choices for the general public and for children over two years of age. The guidelines, a joint publication of the U.S. Department of Agriculture (USDA) and the Department of Health and Human Services (HHS), were written by scientists who searched the scientific literature for studies that give evidence of foods and nutrients that contribute to a healthful lifestyle. The guidelines, developed specifically for the well population, have been published every five years since the first set was put out in 1980. They are not appropriate for people who are sick or who have specific illnesses and may require dietary changes that can be made only in conjunction with a doctor and a registered dietitian.

For the first time, the 2005 guidelines also address physical activity as part of a healthful lifestyle. This is especially important because many diseases are linked to physical inactivity and a poor diet. For instance, the current obesity epidemic has been linked to an energy imbalance: consuming more calories than are used in physical activity.

In a nutshell, the current guidelines encourage individuals to consume a variety of nutrient-dense foods and beverages within and among the basic food groups, while limiting saturated and trans fats, cholesterol, added sugars, salt, and alcohol. In addition, the guidelines recommend adopting an eating pattern balanced with energy needs, as suggested by the USDA MyPyramid.

What Are Healthful Food Choices?

The 2005 Dietary Guidelines describe a healthful diet as "one that

- Emphasizes fruits, vegetables, whole grains, and fat-free or low-fat milk and milk products;
- Includes lean meats, poultry, fish, beans, eggs, and nuts; and
- Is low in saturated fats, trans fats, cholesterol, salt (sodium), and added sugars."

Selected recommendations from the dietary guidelines include . . .

- Eating a variety of foods and beverages within and among the basic food groups while limiting your intake of saturated and trans fats, cholesterol, added sugars, salt, and alcohol.
- Maintaining your weight in a healthy range by balancing calories from foods and beverages with calories expended.
- Engaging in regular physical activity and reducing sedentary activities.
- Eating a sufficient amount of fruits and vegetables while staying within your energy needs.
- Choosing a variety of fruits and vegetables every day.
- Eating three or more whole-grain foods per day.
- Consuming three cups of fat-free or low-fat milk or milk products per day.
- Eating less than 10 percent of your calories from saturated fats, keeping the total fat eaten between 20 to 35 percent of your daily calories.
- Choosing fiber-rich foods often.
- Consuming alcoholic beverages in moderation.

MyPyramid was developed as a visual guide to help individuals fully understand ways to incorporate the Dietary Guidelines into daily eating habits. The MyPyramid Web site, mypyramid .gov, provides many opportunities for individuals to evaluate or to plan what they eat according to the 2005 Dietary Guidelines.

A separate MyPyramid was developed for kids. This visual aid reminds kids and their parents to be physically active each day, or on most days, and to make healthful food choices. Using the MyPyramid worksheet (see sample on page 15) helps people to evaluate their daily intake and plan for better eating habits in the future. This worksheet is useful for parents who want to keep track of their children's diets or for those who may be concerned

A Close Look at MyPyramid  For Kids

MyPyramid for Kids reminds you to be physically active every day, or most days, and to make healthy food choices. Every part of the new symbol has a message for you. Can you figure it out?

Be Physically Active Every Day
The person climbing the stairs reminds you to do something active every day, like running, walking the dog, playing, swimming, biking, or climbing lots of stairs.

Eat More From Some Food Groups Than Others
Did you notice that some of the color stripes are wider than others? The different sizes remind you to choose more foods from the food groups with the widest stripes.

Choose Healthier Foods From Each Group
Why are the colored stripes wider at the bottom of the pyramid? Every food group has foods that you should eat more often than others; these foods are at the bottom of the pyramid.

Every Color Every Day
The colors orange, green, red, yellow, blue, and purple represent the five different food groups plus oils. Remember to eat foods from all food groups every day.

Grains   Vegetables   Fruits   Oils   Milk   Meat & Beans

Make Choices That Are Right for You
MyPyramid.gov is a Web site that will give everyone in the family personal ideas on how to eat better and exercise more.

Take One Step at a Time
You do not need to change overnight what you eat and how you exercise. Just start with one new, good thing, and add a new one every day.

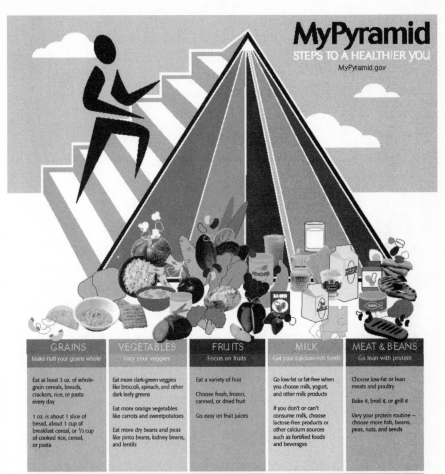

MyPyramid
STEPS TO A HEALTHIER YOU
MyPyramid.gov

GRAINS	VEGETABLES	FRUITS	MILK	MEAT & BEANS
Make half your grains whole	Vary your veggies	Focus on fruits	Get your calcium-rich foods	Go lean with protein
Eat at least 3 oz. of whole-grain cereals, breads, crackers, rice, or pasta every day	Eat more dark-green veggies like broccoli, spinach, and other dark leafy greens	Eat a variety of fruit	Go low-fat or fat-free when you choose milk, yogurt, and other milk products	Choose low-fat or lean meats and poultry
		Choose fresh, frozen, canned, or dried fruit		Bake it, broil it, or grill it
1 oz. is about 1 slice of bread, about 1 cup of breakfast cereal, or ½ cup of cooked rice, cereal, or pasta	Eat more orange vegetables like carrots and sweetpotatoes	Go easy on fruit juices	If you don't or can't consume milk, choose lactose-free products or other calcium sources such as fortified foods and beverages	Vary your protein routine – choose more fish, beans, peas, nuts, and seeds
	Eat more dry beans and peas like pinto beans, kidney beans, and lentils			

For a 2,000-calorie diet, you need the amounts below from each food group. To find the amounts that are right for you, go to MyPyramid.gov.

Eat 6 oz. every day	Eat 2½ cups every day	Eat 2 cups every day	Get 3 cups every day; for kids aged 2 to 8, it's 2	Eat 5½ oz. every day

Find your balance between food and physical activity
- Be sure to stay within your daily calorie needs.
- Be physically active for at least 30 minutes most days of the week.
- About 60 minutes a day of physical activity may be needed to prevent weight gain.
- For sustaining weight loss, at least 60 to 90 minutes a day of physical activity may be required.
- Children and teenagers should be physically active for 60 minutes every day, or most days.

Know the limits on fats, sugars, and salt (sodium)
- Make most of your fat sources from fish, nuts, and vegetable oils.
- Limit solid fats like butter, stick margarine, shortening, and lard, as well as foods that contain these.
- Check the Nutrition Facts label to keep saturated fats, trans fats, and sodium low.
- Choose food and beverages low in added sugars. Added sugars contribute calories with few, if any, nutrients.

MyPyramid.gov
STEPS TO A HEALTHIER YOU

U.S. Department of Agriculture
Center for Nutrition Policy and Promotion
April 2005
CNPP-15

USDA

13

TIPS FOR FAMILIES

EAT RIGHT

1 Make half your grains whole. Choose whole-grain foods, such as whole-wheat bread, oatmeal, brown rice, and lowfat popcorn, more often.

2 Vary your veggies. Go dark green and orange with your vegetables—eat spinach, broccoli, carrots, and sweet potatoes.

3 Focus on fruits. Eat them at meals, and at snack time, too. Choose fresh, frozen, canned, or dried, and go easy on the fruit juice.

4 Get your calcium-rich foods. To build strong bones serve lowfat and fat-free milk and other milk products several times a day.

5 Go lean with protein. Eat lean or lowfat meat, chicken, turkey, and fish. Also, change your tune with more dry beans and peas. Add chick peas, nuts, or seeds to a salad; pinto beans to a burrito; or kidney beans to soup.

6 Change your oil. We all need oil. Get yours from fish, nuts, and liquid oils such as corn, soybean, canola, and olive oil.

7 Don't sugarcoat it. Choose foods and beverages that do not have sugar and caloric sweeteners as one of the first ingredients. Added sugars contribute calories with few, if any, nutrients.

EXERCISE

1 Set a good example. Be active and get your family to join you. Have fun together. Play with the kids or pets. Go for a walk, tumble in the leaves, or play catch.

2 Take the President's Challenge as a family. Track your individual physical activities together and earn awards for active lifestyles at *www.presidentschallenge.org*.

3 Establish a routine. Set aside time each day as activity time—walk, jog, skate, cycle, or swim. Adults need at least 30 minutes of physical activity most days of the week; children 60 minutes everyday or most days.

4 Have an activity party. Make the next birthday party centered on physical activity. Try backyard Olympics, or relay races. Have a bowling or skating party.

5 Set up a home gym. Use household items, such as canned foods, as weights. Stairs can substitute for stair machines.

6 Move it! Instead of sitting through TV commercials, get up and move. When you talk on the phone, lift weights or walk around. Remember to limit TV watching and computer time.

7 Give activity gifts. Give gifts that encourage physical activity—active games or sporting equipment.

HAVE FUN!

MyPyramid Worksheet   Name: _____

Check how you did yesterday and set a goal to aim for tomorrow

Write In Your Choices From Yesterday	Food and Activity	Tip	Goal (Based On a 1800 Calorie Pattern)	List Each Food Choice In Its Food Group*	Estimate Your Total
Breakfast:	Grains	Make at least half your grains whole grains.	**6 ounce equivalents** (1 ounce equivalent is about 1 slice bread, 1 cup dry cereal, or ½ cup cooked rice, pasta, or cereal)		___ ounce equivalents
Lunch:	Vegetables	Color your plate with all kinds of great tasting veggies.	**2½ cups** (Choose from dark green, orange, starchy, dry beans and peas, or other veggies).		___ cups
Snack:	Fruits	Make most choices fruit, not juice.	**1½ cups**		___ cups
Dinner:	Milk	Choose fat-free or lowfat most often.	**3 cups** (1 cup yogurt or 1½ ounces cheese = 1 cup milk)		___ cups
	Meat and Beans	Choose lean meat and chicken or turkey. Vary your choices—more fish, beans, peas, nuts, and seeds.	**5 ounce equivalents** (1 ounce equivalent is 1 ounce meat, chicken or turkey, or fish, 1 egg, 1 T. peanut butter, ½ ounce nuts, or ¼ cup dry beans)		___ ounce equivalents
Physical activity:	Physical Activity	Build more physical activity into your daily routine at home and school.	At least **60 minutes** of moderate to vigorous activity a day or most days.		___ minutes

How did you do yesterday?   ☐ Great   ☐ So-So   ☐ Not So Great

My food goal for tomorrow is: _____

My activity goal for tomorrow is: _____

* Some foods don't fit into any group. These "extras" may be mainly fat or sugar—limit your intake of these.

15

about specific eating problems. Older children may choose to keep their own records.

Some features of the Web site that provide individualized guidance include:

- **MyPyramid Plan:** A quick estimate of what and how much food you should eat from the different food groups according to your age, gender, and level of physical activity.
- **MyPyramid Tracker:** More detailed information on the quality of your diet and your physical activity status by comparing a day's worth of the foods you eat with current nutrition guidelines. It includes nutrition and physical activity advice tailored to your desire to maintain your current weight or to lose weight.
- **Inside MyPyramid:** In-depth information for every food group, including recommended daily amounts in common measures, such as cups and ounces, with specific examples given.
- **Tour MyPyramid:** An animated tour of the new pyramid.
- **Tips and Resources:** Practical ideas that can help you start planning a healthful diet, tips about specific foods in each food group, and definitions and descriptions of different levels of physical activity.
- **For Kids:** MyPyramid material designed specifically for children ages 6 to 11.

Related Internet Links

2005 Dietary Guidelines for Americans
 www.health.gov/dietaryguidelines/dga2005/document

MyPyramid
 www.mypyramid.gov/guidelines

Physical Activity
 www.cdc.gov

Nutrition Facts Label
 www.cfsan.fda.gov

Food Safety Information
 www.fsls.usda.gov/Food_Safety_Education/Food_Safety_
 Education_Programs/index.asp

What Do the Dietary Guidelines and MyPyramid Mean for You and Your Family?

The main message is make a change in lifestyle by . . .

- Changing your eating habits.
- Making wise food choices.
- Increasing daily physical activity.

Changes made today will help you to feel better, look fit, be more productive, and be healthier in the future.

Change Your Eating Habits

Look at the way your family eats during the day and over a week's time. Do you eat on the run? Do the children eat while watching TV or playing computer games? Where do you eat most meals and snacks? How much do you eat? How many times during the day do you eat something? You get the idea—before you can change, you must know what you are currently doing.

Tips for Changing Your Eating Habits

- Make eating one event where you concentrate on the food you eat, not a multitasking event where you are also reading the paper or watching TV. Most of us are unaware of what or how much we eat because we are doing other activities at the same time.
- Taste foods during preparation, but don't make it a snacking event. It's not unusual for some people to consume an entire meal's portion through tasting alone.
- When you eat as a family, with others, or alone, make a place setting to sit, eat, and enjoy. Enjoy the food and then move on to other activities. Plan to eat at specific places, primarily at the kitchen table. Avoid eating in your car. If you must stop at a fast-food restaurant, go in and sit at a table.
- Control the amounts you eat. Look carefully at portion sizes. Supersizing may appear to be an economic bargain

("just ten cents more for twice as much food"), but it can be a nutritional disaster. Portions or serving sizes have grown dramatically over the years as consumers have demanded more and more. Dinner plates have also gotten larger. Try to use smaller plates, like luncheon or salad plates, especially at home, and your portions are likely to be more in line.

- Eat only what you need to feel satisfied, not stuffed. When portions are large, divide them and save some for later. When eating away from home, ask for a box to take leftovers home, or share one portion with other people. Kid-size meals can be purchased for adults.

- Spread your meals and snacks out over the course of a day. Don't skip meals. Make it a point to eat breakfast. This first meal of the day is so important after a night of fasting, or having nothing to eat. Eating in the morning also helps to prevent overeating at midmorning snack time or at the noon meal. Plan for three mealtimes and two snacks throughout the day, with the snacks being lighter than the meals. This will help you avoid too much snacking late at night.

- Eat a variety of foods and all foods in moderation. Overindulging or eating large amounts of one food will usually decrease the variety of foods you eat. You are much more likely to get the daily nutrients that you need by eating many types of food. By choosing to eat only a hamburger and French fries, a person is likely to eat more of each one rather than if he or she sits down to a hamburger, French fries, a tossed salad, and fresh fruit.

- Pack healthful snacks (ready-to-eat raw vegetables and fruits, unsalted nuts, low-fat cheese, or low-fat crackers) when you are on the run to avoid snacking on fast food or on high-fat, high-calorie foods.

Make wise food selections

- Choose grilled, baked, and broiled foods instead of fried foods, and choose steamed vegetables instead of those covered in heavy, creamy sauces. Restaurants offer these alternative preparations—you just have to ask. For instance, request a baked potato (with butter, margarine, or light sour cream on the side) instead of French fries or fried potatoes, baked or broiled fish instead of batter-fried, and grilled or steamed vegetables instead of those covered with sauces.

- Eat lean when choosing meats, and eat fish more often than other kinds of meat. Remove the skin from chicken and discard it.

- Add some nonmeat sources of protein to your meals. Try more dried beans and peas. Add chickpeas, nuts, or seeds to a salad, pinto or black beans to a burrito, or kidney beans to chili or soup.

- Make half of your grains whole. Choose whole-grain foods, such as whole-wheat bread, oatmeal, brown rice, and low-fat popcorn as your grains of choice instead of processed grains. Get into the habit of reading nutrition labels for accurate information.

- Plan for changes in your food choices to be gradual—make small changes, one at a time. For instance, opt to try a new or rarely eaten food once each week to add variety to your diet.

- Use water as the beverage of choice during and between meals. Avoid presweetened or high-calorie soft drinks. Children should learn to drink water as their beverage of choice and not rely on juices, sweetened juice drinks, sports drinks, or soft drinks. Everyone should drink more water in the summertime or during hot weather or intense physical activity that causes perspiration.

- Shop for nutrient-rich foods at the grocery store. Always plan ahead by preparing a list before you go to the supermarket.

- Decrease your consumption of sugars, fats, and salt. Change your choice of oils to those that are more healthful—seek out liquid vegetable oils such as canola, soybean, olive, and corn, while still watching how much you use.

- Eat some colorful fruits and vegetables every day. For instance, choose red or pink grapefruit instead of white;

carrots; sweet potatoes; beets; red, yellow, or orange peppers; blueberries; strawberries; tomatoes; and so on. These richly colored foods contain many compounds that are beneficial to your health.

- Select dark green and leafy vegetables every day. The dark green means that they contain more nutrients. Examples are spinach, various lettuces (the greener the better), and greens (turnip greens, collards, chard, kale).

QUICK BITE

Vary the vegetables you eat every day to get an assortment of nutrients each week.

- Remember to eat some vitamin C–rich fruits every day. Examples are citrus fruits of all kinds (grapefruit, oranges, tangerines, clementines) and other fruits like strawberries, cantaloupe, and tomatoes (you can consider tomatoes either a fruit or a vegetable). Juices of these fruits and vegetables are also good sources of vitamin C.

- Select fruits canned with 100% fruit juice or water instead of syrup.

- Keep fruits and vegetables on hand in a ready-to-eat form and make them accessible to children. All fruits and vegetables need to be washed prior to eating. Cut celery, broccoli, or cauliflower into small pieces for snacking and to eat with dipping sauces.

- Prepare casseroles for dinner. These are often easy to make and will serve as one-dish meals. Include a variety of vegetables in the casserole.

- For desserts, choose fruits in various forms, whether fresh, frozen, or canned.

- If you regularly drink whole milk, try changing to fat-free milk gradually over time. Milk may be purchased in a variety of fat contents. Choose reduced-fat (2%), then low-fat (1%), then fat-free or skim milk and dairy products. For variety, choose low-fat flavored milks or buttermilk. Ask for lattes or cappuccinos with skim milk instead of whole milk. And when cooking with milk, choose fat-free or low-fat options. Children under two years of age should remain on whole milk. Once they reach two years of age, switch to 2% for adequate nutrition and less fat as they grow.

- Low-fat hard cheeses, cottage cheese, sour cream, and yogurt are all good sources of calcium and should be part of the three daily servings of dairy products. They can be eaten with hot cereal or in casseroles and soups to reduce calories. In addition, look for other foods that are fortified with calcium, such as orange and other fruit juices, cereals, and breads.

- If you cannot tolerate milk products, choose calcium-fortified juices, cereals, breads, soy beverages, or other soy products. Fish canned with bones, including salmon, are also good sources of calcium.

> **QUICK BITE**
> Make changes slowly, and they will likely become habits that stick with you.

MyPyramid

Let's look at the food groups found within MyPyramid. It doesn't matter where we start because all groups and individual foods are important. At the end of the day, your goal is to mix the foods you choose from each group, but with emphasis on eating the recommended number of servings and on proper serving sizes. Since most people do not eat enough vegetables, let's start with vegetables.

Vegetable Group

You can eat them raw or cooked, frozen, canned, fresh, or dried/ dehydrated. When you eat vegetables raw, first be careful to wash them thoroughly or scrub them with a vegetable brush under running water. Prepare raw vegetables by cleaning them and putting them into plastic bags while you put away groceries. You and your children are much more likely to snack on raw vegetables if they are clean and ready to eat at any time.

Try vegetables plain or mixed into main dishes or casseroles. Also, try them in stir-fries or added to soups or stews. You can eat more than one serving of vegetables at one time. Add finely shredded carrots or zucchini to peanut butter for a moist sandwich spread or to muffins or meatloaf to increase your consumption of vegetables. Add frozen or fresh broccoli florets to pasta dishes of all kinds, whether with a red or a white sauce.

To maintain a balance of calories, prepare vegetables most often raw, baked, roasted, or steamed rather than fried. Cooking vegetables on the outdoor grill produces a very tasty result and provides variety to a grilled meal. Try slicing the vegetables, spraying the grill with a nonfat cooking spray, and placing the cut vegetables on the grill as individual pieces. Good choices for grilling are eggplant, bell peppers, squash, onions, mushrooms, and so on, in addition to the traditional potatoes and corn on the cob. Other vegetables may be added to kabobs (on a skewer) and grilled—for example, grape tomatoes, pearl onions, and mushrooms.

Do you have trouble getting your children to eat vegetables? Try these tips . . .

- Eat your vegetables in front of them.

- Make a treat with raw vegetables and a low-fat dipping sauce, such as salsa or ranch dressing.

- Encourage children to help with putting together a soup or a salad and making some of the decisions about the ingredients. Young children love to wash lettuce under running water or in the sink and tear and toss a salad with their hands.

- Keep raw veggies ready to eat and available in the refrigerator at all times—carrot strips or baby carrots, celery sticks, grape tomatoes, sweet pepper strips, cucumber slices, and others. (These are vegetables that keep well and do not discolor when sliced raw and stored in plastic bags.)

- Use vegetables as pizza and sandwich toppings.

As in the following list, vegetables are generally grouped together according to color and nutrient content for ease in identifying what you need to eat. Seek out new choices for you and your family.

Vegetable Categories and Varieties

Dark Green Vegetables
bok choy
broccoli
collard greens
dark green leafy lettuce
kale
mustard greens
romaine lettuce
spinach
turnip greens
watercress

Orange Vegetables
acorn squash
butternut squash
Hubbard squash
carrots
pumpkin
orange or yellow peppers
rutabagas
sweet potatoes

Dried Beans and Peas*
black beans
black-eyed peas
garbanzo beans (chickpeas)
kidney beans
lentils
lima beans
navy beans
pinto beans
soybeans
split peas
tofu (bean curd made from soybeans)
white beans

Starchy Vegetables
corn
green peas
lima beans (green)
potatoes

Other Vegetables
artichokes
asparagus
bean sprouts
beets
brussels sprouts
cabbage
cauliflower
celery
cucumbers
eggplant
green beans
green or red peppers
iceberg (head) lettuce
mushrooms
okra
onions
parsnips
tomatoes
tomato juice
vegetable juice
turnips
wax beans
zucchini squash
yellow squash

*MyPyramid includes dried beans and peas as a subgroup of the vegetable group, although they also can fit into the meat and beans group.
Source: MyPyramid.gov

QUICK BITE

Spend a little more and buy prewashed and ready-to-eat vegetables if you will eat these more frequently.

For convenience and to save time, try the fresh-cut or ready-to-eat packaged vegetables now available in the grocery stores. You will find all sorts of salad and cole slaw mixes, as well as spinach and greens (turnip, mustard, and collard greens), in bags. Among other items, baby carrots, celery sticks, broccoli and cauliflower florets, green beans, and green pea pods come ready to eat in packages. They are usually a little more expensive, but they save you time in preparation and can be combined in a number of ways.

How many servings of vegetables should you and your family eat daily or within a week?

The amount needed depends on your age, gender, and level of physical activity, to be specific. In general, however, you need three to four servings of vegetables daily, with the serving size varying depending on your age. For the week, you and each member of your family need one to three cups per week from the dark green vegetable group; one-half to two cups of the vegetables in the orange group; one-half to three cups of dried beans and peas; one and one-half cups from the starchy group; and four to seven cups from the other vegetable group. One cup of vegetable juice is equivalent to one cup of raw or cooked vegetables. For leafy green vegetables, two cups of fresh greens count as the equivalent of one cup of vegetables.

Fruit Group

Fruits may be eaten raw, frozen, dried or dehydrated, or canned. Fruit juices are also encouraged, especially those that contain 100%

QUICK BITE

Aim for 100% fruit juice over presweetened juices, and be careful about how much you consume: one-half cup of juice is a serving.

juice. To maintain caloric balance, choose canned fruits that are canned in juice or packed in water. Fruit canned in light or heavy syrup may be eaten on occasion, but they do contribute more calories from the added sugar in the syrup.

Again, variety is important in the fruit we choose to eat because we generally depend on fruits for most of our daily vitamin C allotment. Citrus fruits are better sources of this vitamin, but every type of fruit provides a variety of vitamins that are important to our health.

All fruits should be washed thoroughly before we eat them, especially if they're eaten raw. The skins of most fruits are edible and are additional sources of fiber. Fruits bought in season are usually less expensive and more flavorful. At other times, almost every fruit is available frozen and canned. Currently available in most supermarkets are fresh-cut fruits, which are convenient and save time. Combinations of these melons or singly packed selections are favorites when in season: cantaloupe, honeydew, and watermelon. Citrus fruits include orange slices, grapefruit slices, and tangerines.

QUICK BITE

Keep a bowl of fresh fruit on a table or counter (or accessible in the refrigerator) for easy snacking.

Eating fruits of every kind should be encouraged. If you buy a variety of fruits, it's easier to get your family to consume the recommended amounts. The following list includes most fruits that are available, some of which come in different varieties, colors, and combinations.

Fruit Categories and Varieties

Individual Servings

apples	grapes	prunes
apricots	nectarines	raisins
bananas	oranges	raspberries
blackberries	peaches	strawberries
blueberries	pears	tangerines
cherries	plums	

Minimal Preparation

avocado	honeydew	mangoes
cantaloupe	kiwi	papayas
cranberries	lemons	pineapple
grapefruit	limes	watermelon

Dried or Dehydrated

apples	cherries	papayas
apricots	cranberries	peaches
bananas	figs	pineapple
blueberries	mangoes	raisins

QUICK BITE

Dried fruits can be combined with nuts and seeds for a trail-mix snack to take with you or to eat at home. Making your own and keeping it in an air-tight container is much more economical than buying the premade mix. It also allows you to use the combinations of fruits, nuts, and seeds that your family will eat.

How much fruit should you and your family eat each day or within a week?

Again, the specific amount depends on your age, gender, and physical activity, with your children needing smaller serving sizes. In general, each family member needs one to two cups of fruit each day or seven to fourteen cups within a week. A cup of fruit, one-half cup of 100% fruit juice, or one-half cup dried fruit is considered a one-cup serving of fruit. This also translates into two to four servings of fruit for a family member each day.

Working fruit into the daily schedule of meals and snacks . . .

- Offer fruit at all meals. For breakfast, use bananas, peaches, blueberries, nectarines, or raspberries on cereal; blueberries or dried cherries in pancakes; or drink 100% orange or grapefruit juice. For lunch, eat a mixture of fruits as a salad or in a salad; add banana slices or raisins to a peanut butter sandwich. For dinner, use grilled or heated fruit as a side dish for all meats; serve fruit salad, a fruit dessert, or pureed fruit sauce to pour over ice cream or frozen yogurt.

- Use low-fat yogurt as a dipping sauce for cut or sliced fresh fruit.

- Add individually frozen fruits (mixed berries, strawberries, peaches) to low-fat milk or buttermilk, and blend the ingredients for a cool drink at snacktime or mealtime. The frozen fruit makes the beverage thick.

- Add fruits such as raisins, dried cranberries, mandarin orange slices, grapes, pears, or apples to tossed vegetable salads.

- When adding sliced white fruits (apples, bananas, pears), sprinkle them with lemon or lime juice to keep them from turning dark.

- Add dried or fresh fruit to muffin mixtures.

- Eat fruit more often than you drink 100% fruit juice, as the fiber content is usually higher and, of course, the portions tend to fill you up more.

Ideas for getting children and other family members to eat fruit . . .

- Set an example by eating fruit daily for meals or snacks.
- Make a fresh fruit cup or single servings of fruit available at all times.
- Pack single servings of fruit in small containers for school meals and picnics.

- Use a trail-mix combination of dried fruits, seeds, and nuts for snacks or as a surprise in school lunchboxes.

QUICK BITE

Let your children select the fruit of the meal to encourage more healthful eating habits.

- Offer dried fruit pieces instead of other sweets for between-meal snacks. Be sure to use the unsugared, noncrystallized dried fruit, as it is a better choice and contains less added sugar.

- Allow children to help select the fruit at the grocery store, prepare the fruit for eating, and arrange the fruit on plates or in bowls for family meals.

Grains and Cereal Group

In previous years, the Food Guide Pyramid called this group cereal and cereal products. Currently MyPyramid points to the importance not only of cereals or grains but of *whole* grains being

even more essential. Whole grains have higher fiber content than do refined or enriched grains and cereals. They also contain B vitamins, iron, and magnesium. Eating whole grains and cereals as part of a complete meal helps to reduce the risk of some chronic diseases.

QUICK BITE

Eat half of your grains as whole.

The current recommendation is that you eat at least half of your cereals and grains as whole-grain products. You and each member of your family need to eat at least three ounces of whole-grain cereal, bread, crackers, pasta, or rice every day.

How do you determine whether a cereal or a grain is a whole grain?

The food ingredient label is key to the identification of whole-grain products. Select foods that list one of the following whole-grain ingredients first on the label's ingredient list: brown rice, bulgur, graham flour, oatmeal, whole oats, whole wheat, whole rye, whole-grain corn, and wild rice. You cannot tell by the color of the product because some breads and cereals contain condiments that add color. In addition, pay attention to the fiber content on the label because the amount of fiber, or the percentage daily value (% DV) of fiber, indicates the amount of whole grain in the product. The greater the amount of fiber, the more likely it has a good amount of whole grain. If you don't choose whole grain, at least be sure that the cereal or grain product is enriched, which means that significant amounts of nutrients have been added back to the grain during processing.

Foods labeled "multigrain," "stone ground," "100% wheat," "cracked wheat," "7-grain," "rye," or "bran" are usually not whole-grain products.

QUICK BITE

Look for the following in the ingredients list for an indicator of a whole-grain food.

bulgur	whole-grain barley
whole rye	whole oats
oatmeal	whole-grain corn
wild rice	whole wheat
brown rice	graham flour

Manufacturers are rapidly changing cereal and grain products available due to the increased interest and demand for whole grains. For instance, there are now white breads made with whole grains, and assorted pastas are now made from whole grains. Reading the label is the only way to know for sure.

How do you identify foods in the grain group?

Food products made from oats, rice, wheat, barley, cornmeal, and rye are included in the grain group. Examples of foods containing grain would be bread, dry or cooked breakfast cereal, tortillas, pasta, rice, and grits. Cereal grains are defined as whole grains or refined grains. Whole grains contain the entire grain kernel, that is, the bran, the germ, and the endosperm. Refined grains have been processed whereby the bran and the germ are removed. This reduces the amount of fiber, iron, and B vitamins in the processed product, which is why these products are enriched (the nutrients lost in processing are added back). Many food products are made from combinations of whole grains and refined grains. Note the definitive classifications in the following list.

Grain Categories and Varieties

Whole Grains	Refined Grains
brown rice	degermed cornmeal
bulgur (cracked wheat)	white bread
oatmeal	white flour
whole cornmeal	white rice
whole-wheat flour	

Common Foods from the Grain Group

Whole Grains	Refined Grains
brown rice	cornbread
buckwheat	corn tortillas
bulgur	couscous
oatmeal	crackers
popcorn	flour tortillas
ready-to-eat cereal	grits
muesli	noodles
whole wheat flakes	pasta
whole-grain barley	macaroni
whole-grain cornmeal	spaghetti
whole-grain tortillas	pitas
whole rye	pretzels
whole-wheat bread	ready-to-eat cereal
whole-wheat buns and rolls	cornflakes
whole-wheat crackers	rice flakes
whole-wheat pasta	white bread
wild rice	white buns and rolls
	white rice

Less Common Whole Grains

amaranth
millet
quinoa
sorghum
triticale

How much whole grain should you and your family eat in a day or within the week?

The recommendations include a minimum amount of fiber that should be consumed daily. You and each member your family

QUICK BITE

To eat more whole grains in your diet select a whole-grain product for a refined product; for example, choose whole-wheat bread instead of white bread.

should aim for three- to six-ounce equivalents of whole grains daily, with minimum recommendations of one-and-a-half- to three-ounce equivalents. Smaller amounts are for young children, and larger amounts are for older children and adults. At least one-half of the grains you eat should be from the whole-grain group. One-half cup of cooked pasta, rice, or cereal; one cup of ready-to-eat cereal; or one slice of bread can be counted as a one-ounce equivalent.

How can you ensure that your family eats the recommended amounts of whole grains?

- For pancakes or baked products, use one-half whole wheat or oat flour instead of white flour.
- Add whole-grain bread or crumbs to meatloaf, burgers, or other meat products.
- Try whole-grain pasta or brown rice in casseroles, soups, or stews.
- Use whole-grain, unsweetened, ready-to-eat cereal for snacks, on top of fruit, or as a topping for frozen yogurt or ice cream.
- As a snack, prepare popcorn without added butter or salt.
- Use whole-grain breads in place of the refined-grain breads you may be currently using.
- Substitute whole-grain baked chips in place of snack foods.

Ideas to entice children to consume greater amounts of whole-grain products . . .

- As with other foods, set a good example. Make sure that whole-grain choices, especially in ready-to-eat cereals, are available.
- Remind children (who are old enough to read) to always study labels to determine whether the product is whole grain.
- Keep whole-grain snack items on hand for between meals.
- Allow children to assist in preparing cooked cereals, pastas, or casseroles using whole-grain products.

Milk, Yogurt, and Cheese Group

Consuming milk and milk products fosters the growth and the maintenance of bones and teeth and reduces the risk of certain chronic diseases such as osteoporosis and hypertension. Milk products are vital for infants, children, and adolescents because of the rapid growth of their bones and teeth and their need to increase their bone density or mass. These benefits are due to the nutrients found in milk products, which include calcium, potassium, vitamin D, and good-quality protein. (If you or a family member is lactose-intolerant, it is crucial that these nutrients be supplied by lactose-free milk products or other types of food. Soy milk is another good alternative.)

QUICK BITE

Choose low-fat or fat-free dairy products whenever you can.

Try to choose low-fat or fat-free options within the milk and milk products food group because most of the fat that naturally occurs in milk products is saturated fat. Overconsumption of these fats can lead to increased cholesterol levels (especially of LDL, the "bad" cholesterol) and increased risk of heart disease. In addition, the low-fat and fat-free choices will have fewer calories, which is so important in helping you and members of your family maintain a healthy body weight. Whole milk and many cheeses contain saturated fats and should be eaten in moderation.

What are examples of foods included in the milk products group?

Fluid milk products and most foods made from milk are included in this group. To belong in this category, the food made from milk must retain a significant calcium content. Examples of foods made from milk that are not included in this group are cream cheese, butter, and cream. To avoid getting too many calories and too much saturated fat, you should choose milk group products that are low in fat. After a child turns two, you should incorporate a low-fat milk (2%) into his or her diet. In later years, it is possible to use 1% or fat-free milk, too.

The following list shows foods that are commonly included in the milk group.

Milk Group Categories and Varieties

Milk

all fluid milk
  buttermilk
  fat-free (skim)
  low-fat (1%)
  reduced-fat (2%)
  whole milk
flavored milks
  chocolate
  strawberry
lactose-free milks
lactose-reduced milks

Cheese

hard natural cheeses
  cheddar
  mozzarella
  Parmesan
  Swiss
processed cheeses
American
soft cheeses
  ricotta
  cottage cheese

Milk-Based Desserts

frozen yogurt
ice cream
ice milk
pudding made with milk

Yogurt

all yogurt
  fat-free
  low-fat
  reduced-fat
  whole-milk

How much should you and your family consume from the milk group?

As with the other food groups, the amount of milk or milk products that is recommended depends on age, with children needing less than other family members do. Children need two to three cups daily, and all other family members need three cups daily. Two ounces of processed cheese or one and one-half ounces of natural cheese are equivalent to one cup of fluid milk.

Ideas to include milk products in your family meals . . .

- Serve milk as a beverage at meals, for yourself and for other members of your family.

- Get in the habit of consuming fat-free milk products on a regular basis. Incorporate fat-free products into your diet gradually. If you currently drink whole milk, try mixing it half and half with 2% milk; then go to 2% altogether; next, dilute the 2% with low-fat; and then repeat this again with fat-free or skim milk. Children under five should continue drinking 2% milk.

- Cook cereals such as oatmeal or rice with milk instead of water.
- Substitute low-fat or skim milk in recipes calling for whole milk—for example, soups, sauces, gravies, or lattes, or other milk beverages.
- Use yogurt for a dipping sauce with fruit.
- Use shredded low-fat cheeses for casseroles, vegetables, soups, pizzas, and so on.
- Try cottage cheese as a topping for baked potatoes.
- Be sure that milk products are safe by buying only those that are pasteurized or made from pasteurized milk.
- Keep milk and milk products refrigerated.
- Use low-fat or fat-free instant dry milk in baked goods, soups, or casseroles.

Tips for getting your children to consume adequate amounts of milk products

- As always, set an example by drinking milk as a beverage with your meals.
- Discourage children from drinking an entire glass of milk before they eat other foods on their plates. They will become too full to eat.
- Prepare smoothies with frozen fruit, yogurt, and low-fat milk.
- Substitute low-fat ice cream or frozen yogurt for creamy, full-fat ice creams.
- Use yogurt or blended cottage cheese as a dipping sauce for raw vegetables.
- Choose calcium-fortified fruit juices, cereals, and breads.

Meat and Beans Group

The meat and beans group is a source of many key nutrients that help you and your family maintain good health. These nutrients are protein, B vitamins (especially niacin, thiamin, riboflavin, and B_6), iron, zinc, magnesium, and vitamin E. Protein is necessary for the growth of bones, muscles, skin, and blood; to build enzymes and hormones; and to provide a source of calories. B vitamins are necessary for the release of energy, the creation of red blood cells, the functioning of the nervous system, and the building of other tissues. Iron carries oxygen in the blood. Zinc is used in many biochemical processes in the body and maintains the integrity of the immune system. Magnesium is used in building bones and in the energy release from muscles. Vitamin E is used as an antioxidant to aid in the absorption of vitamin A and prevent the cell oxidation of fatty acids.

How do you identify foods in the meats and beans group?

The following list shows the different foods that are included in this group.

Meats and Beans Group Categories and Varieties

Meats

game meat
  elk, bison
  rabbit
  venison
lean cuts of beef,
  ham, lamb,
  pork, and veal
Lean ground meat
  beef
  lamb
  pork

Fish

finfish
  catfish
  cod
  flounder
  haddock
  herring
  mackerel
  pollack
  salmon
  sea bass
  snapper
  swordfish
  trout
  tuna
shellfish
  clams
  crab
  crayfish
  lobster
  mussels
  oysters
  scallops
  shrimp
canned fish
  anchovies
  clams
  mackerel
  oysters
  sardines
  salmon
  tuna

Poultry

chicken
duck
eggs
goose
ground turkey or
  chicken
turkey

Dried Beans/Peas

bean burgers
garden burgers
veggie burgers
black beans
black-eyed peas
chickpeas (gar-
banzo beans)
kidney beans
lentils

lima beans
navy beans
pinto beans
soybeans
tofu
white beans

Nuts and Seeds

almonds
cashews

mixed nuts
peanut butter
peanuts
pecans
pumpkin seeds
sesame seeds
sunflower seeds
walnuts

Source: MyPyramid.gov.

How do you know how much is recommended to eat from the meat and beans group?

As with other food groups, the amount recommended for you and members of your family depends on age, gender, and level of physical activity. Choose from a variety of items in this group. Keep serving sizes or portions small. Select the leaner cuts of meat or trim the visible fat and the skin prior to cooking. In general, you and members of your family need between two ounces and six ounces per day, gradually increasing the amounts with age (that is, the smallest portions for young children and the largest for adults). A two-year-old child needs as little as two-ounce equivalents per day, whereas an active adult man needs only six- to six-and-a-half-ounce equivalents daily. It is likely that individuals consume much more than these recommendations. The ounce equivalents are one ounce of meat, poultry, or fish; one-quarter cup cooked dried beans or peas; one egg; one tablespoon of peanut butter; or one-half ounce of nuts or seeds.

General tips for including the meat and beans group in your family meals

- Choose lean cuts of meat, and trim away any visible fat.
- Select the following beef cuts for leanness: top loin and sirloin; chuck shoulder and arm roasts; eye of round; and top and bottom round.
- Choose lean pork cuts: tenderloin, center loin, and fresh ham.
- Choose the leanest cuts of chicken: boneless, skinless chicken breasts or chicken tenders.
- Trim the skin from chicken or turkey prior to cooking.
- Drain any fat that accumulates during cooking.
- Broil, bake, roast, grill, poach, or boil all lean meats instead of frying them.
- Cook dried beans and peas without added fat. Use fat-free chicken broth or bouillon and a teaspoonful of oil for seasoning.
- Use a minimum of breading or flouring when you prepare the lean cuts of meat.
- Select beans for a meatless main dish or a side dish to go with meats.
- Enhance the flavor of salads by adding a few nuts or seeds.

What do you need to know about food safety as it relates to raw meats?

The importance of keeping meats safe for eating cannot be overemphasized.

- Raw meats or poultry should not be prepared with the same utensils or on the same cutting boards as fresh foods such as vegetables or fruits.
- Be sure that cutting boards are thoroughly washed before reusing them for any foods other than raw meats.
- Do not eat raw or partially cooked eggs.
- Fish should not be eaten raw. Meats and poultry must be cooked to temperatures that will kill the organisms that can make you sick.

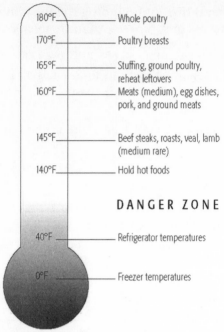

180°F — Whole poultry

170°F — Poultry breasts

165°F — Stuffing, ground poultry, reheat leftovers

160°F — Meats (medium), egg dishes, pork, and ground meats

145°F — Beef steaks, roasts, veal, lamb (medium rare)

140°F — Hold hot foods

DANGER ZONE

40°F — Refrigerator temperatures

0°F — Freezer temperatures

Safe Temperatures for Cooking and Handling Foods

Source: Dietary Guidelines for Americans 2005.

QUICK BITE

Don't take chances. When in doubt about the safety of your food, throw it out.

- Use thermometers to determine the internal temperature of meat before serving it to your family.

- Do not refreeze meats that have been thawed. Cook the meat, and then store it in the freezer.

Oils Group

Oils or fats that are liquid at room temperature make up a very small part of MyPyramid. However, oils contain the essential fatty acids that everyone must have on a daily basis. Most people consume more of the fatty acids than they need from oils in salad dressings or in food preparation, from nuts, or from avocados and some fish. Oils and fats are a concentrated source of calories and therefore should be consumed in moderation to balance your caloric intake.

Common oils that are available for food preparation and often used in commercially prepared foods are cottonseed, canola, corn, olive, safflower, soybean, and sunflower oil.

How much oil is recommended on a daily basis for you and your family?

Daily recommendations for oil range from three teaspoons for two- to three-year-olds to six or seven teaspoons for older children, adolescents, and adults.

How do you know how much oil is contained in the fats that you eat?

The following table shows how much oil is in the fats found in some familiar foods:

OIL EQUIVALENTS IN COMMON FOODS

Food	Oil Content
avocado (½ medium)	3 teaspoons
cashews, almonds, peanuts, dry roasted (1 ounce)	3 teaspoons
peanut butter (2 tablespoons)	4 teaspoons
mayonnaise (1 tablespoon)	2½ teaspoons
margarine, soft (1 tablespoon)	2½ teaspoons
Italian salad dressing (2 tablespoons)	2 teaspoons
sunflower seeds (1 ounce)	3 teaspoons

Discretionary Calories

In MyPyramid, there is a category known as discretionary calories. These calories are needed to balance your daily caloric intake after you have eaten a variety of foods from each food group. The calories may be used for extra or unusual foods that are eaten only occasionally, such as added sugars, alcohol, solid fats, or additional foods from the other food groups. They are to be consumed with discretion.

Added sugars means sugars added to foods during commercial processing or sugar that you add during preparation. Many frequently eaten foods contain these sugars, which add calories without any nutritional benefit. Examples of these "empty calorie" foods are soft drinks, candy, cookies, fruit drinks or punch, cinnamon rolls and other pastries, and sweetened yogurt or milk drinks. Read labels carefully to determine whether the food you eat or drink has added sugars. Watch out for following added sugars:

sugar, brown sugar	fructose
fruit juice concentrate	glucose
honey, molasses	lactose
malt syrup	dextrose
corn sweetener, corn syrup	maltose
high-fructose corn syrup	sucrose
invert sugar, raw sugar	

Increase Your Daily Physical Activity

Regular physical activity is necessary for good health. It can reduce the risk of some chronic diseases and can help you to maintain a healthy weight. Regular activity promotes good balance and gait. You do not have to be an athlete or a super sports person to be healthy—just balance your sedentary activities with those that require more physical exertion, and, over time, gradually increase the low- and moderate-intensity activities. Following are tips for doing just that.

- Balance the energy you take in (calories eaten) with the energy you spend (activity). All physical activity counts, whether it be walking on the sidewalk or on a wooded trail or walking in the home doing housework; recreational activities such as biking, team sports, tennis, golf, working out in the gym, swimming, dancing, jogging, and so on.

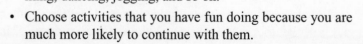

QUICK BITE

Balance calories coming in with calories going out.

- Choose activities that you have fun doing because you are much more likely to continue with them.

- Moderate- or vigorous-intensity activities are encouraged. Examples of moderate activity include biking (fewer than ten miles per hour); yard work or gardening; dancing; golf (if you're walking and carrying clubs); walking quickly (approximately three to three and a half miles per hour); weight training in a light and not lengthy workout. Vigorous activity includes running or jogging (five miles per hour); dancing associated with aerobic exercise; heavy yard or housework; biking more than ten miles per hour; fast walking of more than four miles per hour; basketball; swimming; or vigorous or lengthy weight training. If you currently engage in these activities, continue to do so. If you are not active enough, gradually increase your physical activity. For instance, increase your steps by a hundred a day until you reach a desired number of steps. Increase the amount of time in each exercise or activity by five minutes a day. Gradually, you will work up to the amount of exercise you need on a daily basis. If you lead a sedentary life, set small goals at the beginning and gradually add more activity.

QUICK BITE

The more active you are, the more active your kids will be. It's all about being a good role model.

- When shopping, park farther away from the store and walk. Walk whenever you can instead of riding or driving all the time.
- If you are not regularly active, schedule a specific time (like an appointment) each day for some kind of physical exertion. Start with ten or fifteen minutes at a time and gradually increase it to thirty minutes of moderate to vigorous activity daily.

How do you know if you are exercising or being physically active enough to reach your goals?

Intensity of physical activity is important. The more intense the activity, the less time needed to achieve your goals. The

Dietary Guidelines for Americans recommend that children and adolescents should be involved in sixty minutes of moderate-intensity physical activity daily or on most days. For adults, recommendations are thirty minutes of moderate-intensity physical activity on five or more days or twenty or more minutes of high-intensity physical activity on three or more days.

How often, when, and where should you exercise?

The important thing is to recognize the difference between "inactivity" or sedentary events in your life versus "activity" or exerting yourself physically. Once you identify the inactive times in your life, you can begin to reduce those and concentrate on things that require you to be physically active. Remember, you don't have to exercise in a gym or a classroom setting (although those are great venues for moderate- and high-intensity levels). Almost everything we do requires some physical exertion. Pushing the grocery cart, pushing the infant stroller, walking up stairs instead of taking the elevator, cleaning the house, working in the flower garden or the yard, and walking in the mall will all increase your activity level. *Regularity* is the key word for improving your fitness. Whatever kind of physical activity you do should happen on a regular basis, every day or four or five times a week.

How do you measure the intensity of your physical activity?

The talk test is simple and is generally considered adequate. If you are engaged in a low-intensity physical activity, you should be able to sing along with the activity. Activity at the moderate-intensity level allows you to comfortably carry on a conversation. If you are too out of breath to carry on a conversation or you feel winded, the activity can be considered high intensity.

QUICK BITE

Use the talk test as an indication of workout intensity.

Here are examples of the three levels of physical activity. Remember, *intensity* is the key word. Almost any activity can be high intensity if you really exert yourself for short periods of time.

Intensity Levels of Common Physical Activities

Low Intensity (< 3.5 kcal/min)	Moderate Intensity (3.5 to 7 kcal/min)	High Intensity (> 7 kcal/min)
walking slowly	walking briskly	racewalking, jogging, or running
bicycling, very light	bicycling 5 to 9 mph	bicycling 10 mph
swimming slowly	swimming, recreational water aerobics	swimming laps water jogging
light gardening or pruning	mowing lawn (power mower) raking leaves	mowing lawn (hand mower) heavy or rapid shoveling
dusting, vacuuming	scrubbing floors	moving furniture
conditioning exercise	weightlifting, free weights	intense fitness or marathon training
warming up slow dancing	line dancing aerobic dancing	folk or square dancing step aerobics

For Kids

walking the dog	hopscotch	running,
tag	dodgeball, T-ball	skipping
swimming	skateboarding	jumping rope
bicycling, light effort	horseback riding	roller-skating, fast pace

Tips for parents to motivate and assist their children in transforming from couch potatoes to more active get-up-and-go kids

- Be a role model. "Do as I do, rather than do as I say."
- Participate with your child in physical activities (walking, swimming, leisure-time activities). It helps you cultivate better habits and sustain the activities over a lifetime.
- Keep it fun! Take the dog for a walk. Tumble in the leaves. Play catch. Make up games that require movement. Provide incentives for kids other than food.

- Encourage participation in physical activities at school, including recess, gym, and sports-related opportunities.

- Be sure that the activities are developmentally appropriate for your child. Do not expect the same kind of activity from a three-year-old that you do from a six-year-old. Muscles develop at different ages. The younger child should be encouraged in individual motor-skill games, rather than in competitive group sports.

- Safety in exercise should always come first. For example, insist on helmets when riding bicycles and on knee pads and wrist guards when skating and skateboarding. Remember, the street is usually not the safest place to play, and children will return to places where they have fun.

- Reduce the amount of time that your child is inactive or sedentary. Encourage your child to spend less time watching television, at the computer, or with video games.

- Above all, monitor your child's activities in order to balance his or her sedentary time with energetic games or activities.

- Choose activities that require little or simple equipment. Let children make up the rules and decide how they will participate.

- Plan ahead and make physical activity a regular part of the family program. Devise a schedule that doesn't interfere with school or other activities. Track your activities together each week. Aim for thirty minutes of physical activity for yourself on most days of the week; children should be active sixty minutes every day or on most days of the week.

- Give activity gifts. Choose birthday gifts that inspire activity—maybe a basketball or roller blades, jump rope, or a Frisbee. These gifts will motivate the family to share fun times together.

QUICK BITE
Use MyPyramid.gov to help you improve the quality of your diet, your physical fitness, and more.

3

Planning Ahead

The kitchen is often the hub of the house. We gather there, do homework there, pay bills there, and, of course, eat there. In essence, it's the heart of the home. Everyone wants a nice kitchen; no doubt, it often helps sell a home. We all want the finest cabinets, the flashiest countertops, the most storage, top-of-the-line appliances, and large kitchen tables to gather the troops. We enjoy having nice kitchens, but are we really taking full advantage of them?

Statistics show that more than half of American families today wait until late in the afternoon to decide "What's for dinner tonight?" We live in a fast-paced society. Time is valuable but often is not managed properly. Many days end in disaster at dinnertime. Not only are we at a loss for something to prepare, but once dinner is served, our

QUICK BITE

It takes time to maximize time—a healthful foodstyle and lifestyle takes thought and planning.

QUICK BITE

Problems associated with getting healthful meals on the table for our families are often a result of little or no previous planning or attention to nutritional needs, time limitations, work responsibilities, or lack of food availability.

families give little indication that they enjoyed or appreciated the meal. This becomes the norm more often than the exception. As this continues to happen, we realize that we are getting little satisfaction out of a task that demands so much time and effort. What can we do to manage the situation better?

Many households tend to get in a rut when buying and preparing food. Look at your most frequently prepared meals. Look at the foods you buy at the supermarket—the same ones, time and again. Most people cannot remember the top twenty meals they make at home because the same meals tend to be repeated over and over. Sometimes this is because they are easy to prepare and require little thought. Other meals have a good track record of family acceptance so we tend to rely on them too often. But as complaints about having the "same old thing" continue, we should realize why we need variety and new food choices.

QUICK BITE

An important reason to prepare meals and eat at home is to incorporate fruits, vegetables, and whole grains into the meal; often, these foods are lacking in meals eaten away from home.

You need to establish a routine for planning your weekly meals. This will save time in the long run and will thwart the frustration that accompanies meal preparation and acceptance. The goal is serving delicious, healthful meals that your family anticipates and enjoys—a win-win opportunity for everyone.

Developing a healthful foodstyle does require some planning. The government, the media, and the press have besieged us to take ownership of our bodies. With so many self-made nutrition experts and fad diets, it is difficult to know what to eat or how to make the right choices. Learning to select and prepare food is essential. Refer back to chapter 2 on the 2005 Dietary Guidelines and

QUICK BITE

Learn to take ownership of your health and your food intake.

QUICK BITE

Set your family's
expectations. Develop
your own food and
nutrition rules, and
encourage the family
to stick with them.

MyPyramid as you plan meals, or
seek assistance from your physician
or registered dietitian (RD). They
cannot give you advice that will
guarantee good health, but they can
guide you on the pathway toward it.
Keep this in mind as you decide on
the best options for you and your
family.

Creating your personal plan

- First, set goals for your family. What would you like to accomplish? You have to start somewhere, but start simply, then progress over time. For example, your first goal could be to clean out your recipe drawer, file, or folder. Next, you could clean out and organize your pantry. Another idea is to create a cycle menu for Monday through Friday each week, by preplanning specific meals for weekdays and avoiding the frustration of last-minute throw-together meals (see our example on page 84). These tasks will definitely help you to plan better.

- Next, look at the coming week's schedule. With one or two busy nights ahead, it's in your best interest to assign tasks to family members. Preplan who is responsible for setting the table, preparing the salad, cutting up fresh fruit, and cleaning up after the meal.

QUICK BITE

Set your dinner
table early in the
day if you have
more time then.

- To avoid last-minute scrambling on hectic nights, you can store previously prepared dishes in your freezer or refrigerator, then thaw and heat them for quick homemade dinners.

- When the staples are in short supply at home, you may need to incorporate ready-to-eat food into your meal. Stop at the grocer's salad bar for cut-up fruit or a prepared salad, or pick up bagged salads or a precooked rotisserie chicken.

- If an occasional stop at a local restaurant seems like the only option, go for it. No meal plan should be so rigid that it precludes your family from experiencing outside activities. Just keep these occasions to a minimum because spontaneous trips to restaurants can be less healthful overall and can strain your budget.

- Keep your favorite recipes handy. When your family approves of a new dish that you try, you may feel like framing the recipe, but it's better to put it into a notebook, a binder, or a file that is easily accessible. Note the ingredients that need to be on hand, and make this dish (and its ingredients) part of your regular collection.

QUICK BITE

Keep a current recipe file. If you haven't prepared a dish in more than three years, throw out the recipe. Update the yearly file and add categories such as quick dishes, family favorites, and slow-cooker meals.

- Prepare a list of entrees, vegetables, and desserts that your family enjoys. Always look for new items to add to this list. Get everyone involved in food preparation. Remember, it's not just Mom's job!

- Sometimes, if one member of the household is at home while the others are away, that person can begin advance dinner preparations if recipes are available and staples are on hand. Preparing familiar dishes also helps family members understand how to put the meals together.

- Take inventory of the freezer, the refrigerator, and the pantry weekly to make sure that necessary items are available. Post shopping lists so that you can jot down what should be on hand and what needs to be bought. Everyone can contribute to this responsibility. When an item runs out, add it to the list immediately.

- Remember, the best way to interest kids in trying new foods is to let them make decisions about food and let them prepare meals.

- Go through your recipes for the week ahead and make sure all the ingredients needed for the upcoming week are listed so that you won't have to scramble for last-minute substitutions.

Organizing Your Recipe Collection

You probably have a drawer, a folder, or a file filled with recipes somewhere in your kitchen. This collection was most likely created over time from magazine and newspaper clippings, as well as from favorite foods of friends and family members. Perhaps every time you used a recipe in your collection, you vowed to create a more usable system. Now is the time to do it.

- Decide how best to store your recipes. Begin with a binder, a book, a notebook, an accordion folder, or a file box.

- Decide when to add and when to discard recipes. A good plan is to try recipes first before placing them in the file. If they pass the family taste test, add them. If any alterations were made to the recipe, write down the changes right away. If you don't make a recipe again for three years, it's time to discard it.

- Label categories in your file. Decide whether you like to categorize by food group (meat, chicken, side dishes, desserts) or whether you prefer categories like quick meals, family favorites, thirty-minute meals, and holiday selections.

- Remember, most families have about fifteen to twenty frequently eaten meals. Try to move beyond this number. Try new foods and add new recipes to your collection, and make them regularly. This will keep everyone happy.

QUICK BITE

Learning to cook is a necessary and important skill.

Stocking Up

Make a list and check it twice! Now with a complete plan and an inventory of what's on hand, prepare your shopping list. Without a list, we sometimes forget to buy items we need or are guilty of

QUICK BITE

Keep a notepad in your kitchen for family members to jot down needed items or supplies as they run out.

purchasing items that we don't need or even things we didn't realize we already had at home. Stocking and organizing a pantry, a refrigerator, and a freezer properly helps to ensure that we will always have ingredients on hand to make family meals. This impulse buying results in wastefulness and strains the budget.

Be aware of the advertised specials from newspapers or in your favorite food market. Sometimes, with a little change or modification to a recipe, these items can be incorporated into your meal plan. Clipping coupons for items you may need will also save you money. Keep in mind, however, that coupons are good only if you regularly use the featured items. Don't buy a product only for the sake of saving a few pennies. Oftentimes, the generic or store brand of the same product may be a better bargain than the name-brand item is, even when bought with a coupon.

QUICK BITE

Remember, a bargain is a bargain only if it can be used in your meal plan!

Your Shopping List

Keeping a shopping plan and a list helps you to plan meals. Create a list that works for you. Make copies to use week after week, either by copying the original or keeping the file on your computer. You can even write in staple items on a regular basis so that you won't forget to purchase them. Post your list in a central location (on the refrigerator or inside the pantry door) so that all family members can add to it.

QUICK BITE

Healthful shopping starts with smart shopping.

My Shopping List

Produce

vegetables
fruits
other

Fresh Meats

beef
poultry
seafood
pork
other

Refrigerated Foods

dairy/yogurt/cottage
 cheese/milk
eggs
margarine
breads
other

Frozen Foods

meats
vegetables
packaged items
frozen yogurt or sherbet
breads
other

**Breads/Grains/Starches/
 Pasta/Rice**

whole-grain breads
bagels
English muffins
flat breads and tortillas
pasta
rice
other

**Convenience/Packaged
 Foods/Snack Foods**

Canned/Jar Foods

Oils/Fats/Sweets

**Dressings/Condiments/
 Beverages/Other Foods**

**Household Items/
 Paper Goods**

Beauty/Toiletries

QUICK BITE

When preparing your shopping list, keep the foods listed
in categories and build your list according to the layout
of the store. This will save time and prevent impulse
buying. You will soon notice that it takes less time to
keep a shopping list than to return to the store for
forgotten items.

What are some good points to remember when stocking up?

- Carefully check the staple items and condiments you need to prepare upcoming meals. It's truly frustrating to be in meal preparation mode, have your recipes laid out, and then find that a particular condiment or staple item (such as flour, sugar, etc.) is not available. Don't we all hate running to the grocery store just for eggs or baking soda?

QUICK BITE

If you run out of an item while cooking, immediately jot it down on your next week's shopping list.

- As you plan your route through the supermarket, visit the frozen foods last. You don't want to pick up frozen yogurt early during your shopping trip only to find it melted by the time you finish.

- Watch for seasonal choices of produce and seasonal best buys. For example, apples, pears, grapes, and citrus fruits may be more of a bargain and be more plentiful in the fall and the winter, while strawberries, melons, and tomatoes may be better to buy in the spring and summer months.

- Precut vegetables, ready-to-use salad mixes, and refrigerated mashed and precut potatoes are great time savers, although they do cost more. Determine which is the best option for your needs. If you hate to wash and cut up a salad or you don't have time, precut vegetables are your best option. It is worth spending a few more dollars to eat healthfully.

- Frozen chopped onions and refrigerated chopped garlic are always great to have on hand. They add flavor to many meals and keep well in the refrigerator and the freezer. Remember, though, to check the "sell-by" date to ensure freshness.

- Buy canned goods, like vegetables, fruit, or even broths, when they're on special. They last a long time and can be available for fixing quick meals in a flash.

The Healthful Kitchen

Use the following list of staples as a guide to building your own. Watch for store specials, especially for nonperishable items such as jarred foods, pastas, cereals, and so on, and buy a little extra.

Start with the starches

- Breads: keep a variety on hand (whole-grain, raisin, tortillas, bagels, pita, English muffins, breadsticks, rolls, buns)
- Pasta (in a variety of shapes and sizes, whole-grain)
- Couscous
- Rice (white, brown, long grain, wild)
- Dry cereals (unsweetened, whole-grain, high fiber)
- Hot cereals (oatmeal, quick and instant, cream of wheat)
- Pretzels, crackers, popcorn (low-fat varieties, too)
- Potatoes (white, sweet)
- Cookies (low-fat, including fig bars, gingersnaps, vanilla wafers, graham crackers)
- Rice cakes
- Baked chips (tortilla, potato)
- Frozen waffles, pancakes, bagels, English muffins

Add some protein

- Eggs
- Cheese (low-fat, shredded, cheese sticks, Parmesan)
- Deli meat (turkey, roast beef, chicken, ham, low-fat salami and bologna)
- Dried or canned beans (pinto, black, navy, kidney, garbanzo), legumes
- Peanut butter
- Soups, soup mixes
- Pudding mixes
- Canned or vacuum-sealed tuna or salmon
- Cottage cheese, ricotta cheese (low-fat)

- Yogurt, frozen yogurt, cream cheese, sour cream (low-fat or nonfat)
- Milk (low-fat, skim, 2%, soy, chocolate)
- Dry powdered milk
- Skinless, boneless chicken breasts
- Fresh and frozen fish (whitefish, turbot, fillet of sole, salmon)
- Vegetarian burgers
- Lean ground beef and ground turkey
- Lean cuts of beef (flank, sirloin, tenderloin)
- Lean cuts of pork (canned, cured, boiled ham, Canadian bacon, pork tenderloin)

Add variety with vegetables and fruit

- Canned tomatoes, tomato sauce, tomato paste
- Pasta sauces
- Salsa
- Canned vegetables (green beans, corn, peas, water chestnuts, mushrooms)
- Canned fruit (mandarin oranges, pineapple, peaches, pears—all packed in unsweetened juice)
- Frozen fruit (strawberries, raspberries, blueberries)
- Frozen vegetables (green beans, broccoli, cauliflower, peas, corn)
- Applesauce (unsweetened)
- Jam/fruit spreads
- Fresh fruit (apples, bananas, grapes, berries, pears, oranges, melons)
- Fruit juice (100% juice in a variety of flavors—grape, orange, grapefruit, apple)
- Lemon juice (frozen or canned)
- Fresh vegetables (carrots, celery, cucumbers, peppers, tomatoes, cherry tomatoes, broccoli, cauliflower, onions, green onions, lettuce varieties, spinach)
- Dill, bread and butter, sweet, or sour pickles

And all the extras

- Mustard/Dijon mustard
- Ketchup
- Soy sauce, teriyaki sauce, barbecue sauce
- Salad dressings (low-fat), bottled or dried
- Mayonnaise, flavored mayonnaise (light)
- Oils (olive, vegetable, cooking spray)
- Bread crumbs
- Sugar (brown, white)
- Flour (white, whole wheat)
- Salt, pepper

QUICK BITE

If containers of flour or cornstarch are too large for storage, place the flour or cornstarch in airtight, resealable plastic bags to store.

- Vinegars (white, rice, balsamic, flavored)
- Baking powder, baking soda
- Cornstarch
- Chili powder
- Cocoa powder (unsweetened)
- Spices/herbs of choice
- Extracts (vanilla, almond, mint)
- Coffee/tea
- Bouillon cubes or granules

QUICK BITE

Must-Have Foods

Chicken breasts, salmon, tuna, canned beans, carrots, sweet potatoes, dark green vegetables, fresh berries, apples, oranges, whole-grain breads, low-fat dairy.

Reading and Understanding
Nutrition Food Labels

Nutrition Facts food labels are your main source of information about what you eat; they provide you with facts on the nutrients contained in each food you purchase. Labeling guidelines on food products are regulated by the U.S. Food and Drug Administration, while the U.S. Department of Agriculture governs the labels that are found on fresh meat and poultry products. Federal laws require foods to carry Nutrition Facts food labels on every product that is packaged or processed.

Nutrition Facts labels provide consumers with up-to-date information on the contents of particular foods. Current nutritional research is the source of this information. Beginning in 2006, manufacturers were required to add information about trans fats to all food labels. This requirement stemmed from consumer interest and recent research about the effects of trans fats on health. Trans fats are typically found in fried foods, potato chips, cookies, crackers, pastries, and margarine. Research has shown that a person's risk of heart disease is increased from consuming foods with trans fats, as this type of fat tends to raise one's bad cholesterol levels (LDL—low-density lipoproteins).

QUICK BITE

The information contained on the Nutrition Facts label provides helpful facts about the nutritional content of the food you feed your family.

Even though a label indicates that a particular food has no trans fats, consumers need to be aware that the food could still contain other harmful fats, such as saturated fats. The entire label is important, not just one aspect of it. A sample of a food label can be found on page 57. Learn to understand what items on each line mean.

Other important information found on Nutrition Fact labels is the recommended serving size, the number of servings per container, the number of calories in one serving, the number of calories from fat in a serving, and the amount of nutrients per serving, including total fat, saturated fat, cholesterol, sodium, total carbohydrates, dietary fiber, sugars, and protein. Amounts of these nutrients are listed in grams and milligrams per serving, as well as in percentages of Daily Values. Daily Values are also

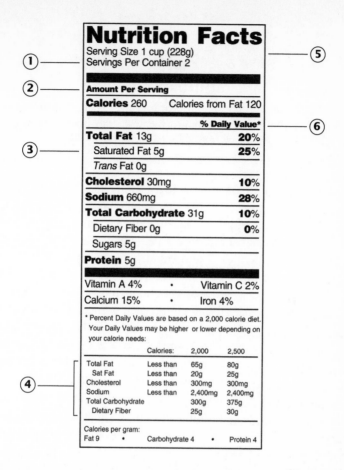

Nutrition Facts

Serving Size 1 cup (228g)
Servings Per Container 2

Amount Per Serving

Calories 260　　Calories from Fat 120

	% Daily Value*
Total Fat 13g	**20%**
Saturated Fat 5g	**25%**
Trans Fat 0g	
Cholesterol 30mg	**10%**
Sodium 660mg	**28%**
Total Carbohydrate 31g	**10%**
Dietary Fiber 0g	**0%**
Sugars 5g	
Protein 5g	

Vitamin A 4%	•	Vitamin C 2%
Calcium 15%	•	Iron 4%

* Percent Daily Values are based on a 2,000 calorie diet.
Your Daily Values may be higher or lower depending on
your calorie needs:

		Calories:	2,000	2,500
Total Fat	Less than		65g	80g
Sat Fat	Less than		20g	25g
Cholesterol	Less than		300mg	300mg
Sodium	Less than		2,400mg	2,400mg
Total Carbohydrate			300g	375g
Dietary Fiber			25g	30g

Calories per gram:
Fat 9　　•　　Carbohydrate 4　　•　　Protein 4

① Servings Per Container: refers to the number of servings found in this container.

② Amount Per Serving: refers to the nutrient content for each serving of food.

③ Saturated Fat/Trans Fat: keep your eye on saturated fats and trans fats—these fats have been found to raise (LDL) bad cholesterol and increase overall risk of heart disease.

④ This section lists the recommended daily limits of fat, saturated fat, cholesterol, and sodium, plus amounts of carbohydrates and fiber a person should aim for on a daily basis for diets of 2,000 and 2,500 calories.

⑤ Serving Size: refers to the amount or the portion a person should eat at one time.

⑥ % Daily Value: is based on a 2,000 calorie daily diet. These values may be higher or lower, based on the number of calories in the diet. Each person should aim for 100% each day of total carbohydrate, dietary fiber, vitamins, and minerals and not exceed 100% for total fat, sodium, and cholesterol.

QUICK BITE

A Daily Value found on a Nutrition Facts label indicates the percentage of a particular nutrient one should strive for based on an average 2,000-calorie daily diet.

required for vitamins A and C and the minerals calcium and iron.

Federal law also requires that food manufacturers list all ingredients found within each food item. This information helps interested consumers but is also especially useful for individuals who have food allergies or intolerances, special dietary needs, or religious restrictions. These ingredients, listed in descending order by weight, include all the substances found within each particular food item.

QUICK BITE

Ingredients on a food label are listed in descending order by weight.

The Nutrition Facts label gives consumers the information they need to make wise choices about the food they eat and feed their families. For individuals seeking to modify their weight or watch the weight of family members, this information lists caloric and fat values, which can be so important to weight control.

At the very bottom of each Nutrition Facts label is information on target daily values for adults based on both a 2,000- and a 2,500-calorie diet. Daily limits for the nutrients—fat, saturated fat, cholesterol, and sodium—are listed, as well as the appropriate intake for total carbohydrates and dietary fiber.

Not only is reading and understanding Nutrition Facts labels important for adults, but children should be encouraged to do so as well. You'll be amazed at how children respond to this helpful information, as they learn more about the foods they eat.

Making Time to Shop

Shopping should be a pleasure, not a chore! Of course, many people today don't have much time to shop. Maybe they don't enjoy the task either. We will try to make it as pleasant as possible for you. Remember, you must start with a list and a plan.

Since our hectic lives are our greatest obstacle, making time to shop requires some discipline. Designating enough time and adhering to budget restrictions are probably the most important elements of the shopping trip. Remember, successful shopping can determine whether mealtime is a success or a failure.

Decide when and where to shop. Weekly ads usually come out right before the weekend, so this is when you'll find the best bargains. Usually, by late Sunday night, store shelves are getting bare and bargains are in short supply. Many perishable foods start to dwindle and may not look fresh. Over the weekend, stores begin to restock for the week ahead, so Sunday night might not be your best option for shopping. In some cases, you may need to shop in more than one market due to food preferences or according to where preferred items can be purchased freshest. As time goes on, you should be able to figure out the best time to shop—morning, evening, or weekends.

Be savvy with your grocery shopping

- Check weekly flyers and specials. Plan your meals around sale items.
- Buy produce in season.
- Use coupons, but only for necessary items.
- Think frozen and canned for times when fresh foods are not an option.
- Buy whole when you can. A whole chicken cut up is less expensive than cut up pieces.
- Plan for your leftovers. Make extra food to have available for another meal.
- Look for store brand and generic items. Oftentimes, they are the same quality but much cheaper.
- Make meals from scratch whenever you can. Convenience foods cost more but are good in a pinch.
- Maximize your summer. Visit local farmers' markets for fresh foods and good deals.
- Read store shelf labels to determine the best values per serving.

Time-saver shopping tips

- Shop in the same store every week. This will allow you to learn its layout while focusing on the job at hand (store maps are usually available; just ask). Become familiar with your favorite store. Compose the list in an order that lets you begin at the front of the store and progress through the aisles. Back-tracking is not only time consuming, it's also a nuisance. It can waste time and increase your impulse buying.

- Arrange the items on your list that are found in the same generalized areas—for example, fruits and vegetables—to save time. Create a list at home that works for you and add to it weekly. (See our previous example.)

QUICK BITE

Do your grocery shopping after eating a meal. If you shop when you're hungry, you tend to spend more because all food looks tempting.

- Have coupons and specials listed and organized so that you can make quick decisions while shopping. And be a smart shopper by comparing prices to generic or store brands whenever possible.

- Always keep staples on hand. This will help you stay on the right track and will keep your kitchen full of healthful food to feed your busy family.

What the Future Holds

Let's look to the future. Supermarkets are striving to make shopping a more pleasurable experience. They will do what it takes to entice customers into the store. Even though stores are in the business to make a profit, they are aware that time and budget restrictions are important elements to you, the shopper.

Plans are currently underway to make grocery carts more intelligent by equipping them with computers. One of these, the "shopping buddy," is already showing up in grocery stores. This small computer can be installed on the grocery cart to help shoppers find the correct aisle for an item, organize their trip through the supermarket, and keep a running tally of their purchases—anything it takes to make it easier for the consumer.

Personal Shopping Cards

Since many grocery chains already have preferred customer cards, this will easily complement the system. Many people don't realize that these cards aren't just to give you the "preferred price" of an item, but also to record your favorite purchases and keep records and data for the various grocery stores. Personal information about shoppers, such as shopping habits and frequently purchased foods, can be stored on preferred shopping cards. Coupons are also dispersed for common purchases. From this information, stores are able to create databases to analyze what people are buying and what they're not, as well as to determine consumers' overall shopping trends. Information will soon be available that will help customers in other ways—for example, by reminding them to restock staples or to note a current sale on a commonly purchased item.

In the near future, it may be possible to use your home computer to create a shopping list, which is definitely key in getting customers in and out of stores as quickly as possible. Then, in the store with your preferred customer card, you will be able to plug in your name, number, and card, and all of your favorite items will log into this system to help organize your trip through the aisles. This will make your shopping experience faster and more efficient.

Shopping Online

It's no surprise that grocery shopping has joined with other types of online shopping as being a popular and time-saving move for busy consumers. The popularity of these Internet sites will likely increase even further in the future. Sitting down in front of the computer at home or in the office, day or night, and placing a grocery order appeals to many people; however, a number of individuals will still feel the need to pick out their own foods by touching, smelling, and squeezing them. Other people like to comparison shop to get the best deal. Online grocery shopping will work for some individuals but not for others.

So many new shopping experiences will be available in the not-so-far-off future. Keep your eye on these and other opportunities that may show up in a supermarket near you.

4

Make Mealtime Family Time

Back in the mid 1900s, dinnertime meant family time. Dads came home from work in time for dinner, moms prepared hot meals, kids took breaks from homework, and no one had extracurricular activities scheduled through the dinner hour. The family even helped clean up. For many families today, those days are obsolete.

According to recent surveys, more than half of all American families are not even together at dinner. Where is everyone? Where are they going? What are they doing? Oftentimes, moms or dads work late, and kids spend time after school at sports-related practices or part-time jobs. Everyone is running in a different direction. And when family members do return home, they reheat a leftover, pop a convenience food into the microwave, or grab whatever is available. Dinner is often a free-for-all. Can this even be considered dinner? No wonder we live in such a crazed society!

QUICK BITE

Families who share meals together tend to eat more healthfully overall.

Moms often feel guilty when they don't have time to fix home-cooked meals. We intend to help you use shortcuts to feed your family and feel good about it. Many families feel as if they just don't have time to cook, there's no time to prepare, and there's no time to plan ahead. Yet family meals shouldn't be only about the food; there is so much more to them.

In recent years, experts have reported that family mealtime is worth revisiting. Why?

- Family mealtime helps to build stronger family bonds.
- Family mealtime gives family members a chance to talk, share experiences, and enjoy one another's company.
- Family mealtime allows children to learn and to model their behavior after adults whom they look up to, in terms of both social skills and eating habits.
- Family mealtime provides an opportunity to balance food choices by featuring a variety of nutritious foods.
- Family mealtime is an opportunity for family members to learn about and understand traditions and cultural influences that have been passed down.
- Family mealtime influences children positively so that they have a decreased incidence of problems associated with drugs and alcohol.
- Family mealtime fosters qualities in children that lead to greater success in school.

QUICK BITE

There is no greater satisfaction than a family enjoying a healthful meal together.

QUICK BITE

Parents are their kids' best teachers. Parents should help kids learn about healthful foods, healthful habits, and healthful lifestyles.

Bringing Families Together, One Meal at a Time

Food is actually secondary to the importance of family members being together. Sitting around the table, talking with one another, and sharing stories and experiences is key in building healthy family relationships. Yes, it's great to add a nutritious meal to the

QUICK BITE

Make mealtime family time by promoting good eating and lifestyle habits. Teach kids that sharing meals together is a necessary part of being a family.

mix, but when time is limited, it's more important for everyone to come together, eat a delivered pizza along with a tossed salad and fresh fruit, and enjoy the experience of being a family.

So, how can you do this when everyone in the family has his or her own agenda? Family members come and go as they please. First, start small. Think once or twice a week. Work around conflicting schedules. Try a weekend night at first, then add a weekday. If dinnertime is too difficult, plan a lunch or even a breakfast. There are twenty-one meals each week; at least one or two should work for everyone. It may be tough to find an hour for people to get together, so start with fifteen to twenty minutes. Once members of your family come together and experience the benefits of a meal together, they may actually look forward to the next one.

After you've made the commitment to convene for meals, try to maximize the experience.

- Be creative. If Johnny has a late-afternoon baseball game, gather up everyone in the family for a picnic in the park prior to the game. Pick up some chicken or, better yet, make it at home, add cole slaw and fresh fruit, and enjoy your time together outdoors.

- Think ahead. Try to incorporate everyone's favorite dishes into the meal. Maybe have Sara's favorites on Sunday, Frankie's on Friday. It's amazing how kids will want to show up if they know you are serving their favorite dishes.

- Give older children a day to plan a meal for themselves. There's no better way to learn. Let them select a menu and post it for all to see. Have them start by making hamburger patties, putting potatoes in the oven, or even just setting the table. After a while they can progress to preparing more components of the meal. Someday you may find that they have learned so much, they may want to cook an entire meal themselves.

- Use fast-food establishments to your advantage. Fast food doesn't have to be all about fried foods eaten in the car. Pick up a salad or sandwiches at a fast-food restaurant or stop at a grocery store salad bar to add to your dinner meal when you're pressed for time and need variety.

- Avoid distractions at meals. Keep the television off and avoid answering the telephone, including the children's cell phones. Younger children will learn from this, and your time together will be so much more valuable.

- Keep food simple. Don't feel as if you need to plan extravagant meals when everyone comes together. Even a meal as simple as grilled chicken and corn on the cob or vegetable soup and grilled cheese sandwiches is appreciated.

- Encourage kids to cook. The more they do it, the more recipes they'll want to try and the more cooking techniques they'll learn. Kids grow up before you know it. Giving them opportunities to help in the kitchen will provide them with skills they need to manage on their own.

- Think outside the box. Instead of always serving meals in the kitchen, set the dining room table occasionally for a change of pace. It's amazing how well-mannered your kids will become in the dining room. Or arrange a backyard picnic or barbecue. Everyone loves eating outside.

- Let kids serve themselves. They are more able to judge the amount they want to eat. You may even be surprised at some of their food choices.

- Keep mealtime discussions fun. Ask everyone about his or her day. Avoid lecturing, disciplining, or criticizing during the meal. Tell funny jokes and stories, and give everyone a chance to contribute. The more your family gets used to this structure, the better the dinner discussions will be.

- Involve family members of all ages. Everyone should participate in discussions at the table, and should learn to contribute in some fashion to the meal. Devise schedules for setting the table, preparing foods, pouring beverages, and cleaning up—whatever it takes. Everyone should have a job.

- Be a role model. Kids will model their behavior from the adults at the table. If adults don't eat a variety of foods, kids won't either. If adults don't help clean up, neither will the children. If adults use good language, so will the kids. If adults get up to answer the telephone, it won't be long before the kids do it, too. Show your children the proper behavior. In years to come, you will be glad you did.

QUICK BITE

Learn to experience special times and memories by cooking meals together and eating together. Everyone involved will develop a greater appreciation for food and for loved ones.

Handling Picky Eaters

It happens in every home. It's common among all families: dealing with picky eaters. Most likely, picky eaters belong to the younger set, but it's not unusual for older members of the family to be picky as well. Often, it is easier to give in to requests rather than push for change. How can you tackle this issue before it controls you?

First, examine your own eating habits. If you are a picky eater, you may be the reason your children are also picky. If you can understand how your behavior influences your children, you may decide that it is worth changing.

Children learn what they see. When they observe good manners, they develop good manners; when they see adults eating junk food, they develop a liking for junk food; and when they see their parents choosing a variety of nutritious foods, they learn to make wise choices themselves.

All people have favorite foods, as well as foods they don't like. If certain foods aren't enjoyed by the parents, then these foods will probably not show up on the dinner table for the children to sample. As a result, the children won't develop a taste for them, either. It can be a vicious cycle.

Children are notorious for developing food jags, repeatedly requesting the same food over and over—for example, choosing macaroni and cheese night after night or asking for peanut butter and jelly every day. Oftentimes, these foods are not bad choices, and it's likely that mom or dad will tire of the choices long before a child does. Don't be too concerned. There's no harm in repeating the same foods, just try to incorporate variety in accompanying side dishes.

> **QUICK BITE**
>
> It's likely that parents will get tired of children's food jags long before they do. In most cases the foods are healthful selections.

How to tackle a food jag . . .

- Start by making small changes that your child won't notice; for example, try a different bread for the peanut butter and jelly sandwich, or substitute applesauce for the jelly.

- Change the foods that accompany the commonly chosen food; that is, if you always serve carrot sticks with the macaroni and cheese, try cherry tomatoes, or if you always make pepperoni pizza, prepare a veggie pizza instead.

- If your child is determined to eat the same breakfast cereal day after day, mix two breakfast cereals together, first at a ratio of three-quarters to one-quarter, then opting for half and half.

- Think long-term. As your child gets older, his food preferences will likely change. He'll outgrow his love for peanut butter and jelly sandwiches long before he graduates from college and moves into the real world.

The more opportunities your child has to experience different types of foods and flavors, the more likely he will develop a taste for variety. Make mealtime fun, exciting, inviting, and pleasant. All of these factors promote a long-term love for foods.

When offering new foods to your family . . .

- Set a good example by eating the food yourself.

- Let children help with preparation of the new food, allowing them to touch, smell, and taste the food in advance.

- Offer new foods when children are most hungry, at the beginning of the meal.

- Present new food selections with other familiar and favored food choices.

- Don't force or bribe your child to eat a new food; just keep offering it. Sometimes it takes ten to twelve offerings of a food before a child will taste and accept it.

- Start with small portions, then add more as requested.

Comparable Substitutions

If your child rejects one food, you can substitute others. See the following list of comparable substitutions.

If your child doesn't like	Try	Why?
red meat	chicken, turkey, fish, pork, peanut butter, eggs, beans, tofu	more widely accepted; easier to chew
green vegetables	red, orange, yellow vegetables, sweet potatoes, squash, carrots, corn	not as bitter
cooked vegetables	raw vegetables with a dip	more fun

If your child doesn't like	Try	Why?
any vegetable	fruit—apples, bananas, grapes, melon, berries, oranges	sweeter, more widely accepted
milk	yogurt, cottage cheese, pudding, flavored milk—chocolate, strawberry	good calcium sources

What if your child is not eating at all?

On some occasions, a child doesn't even seem hungry. This can be very frustrating to any parent, especially one who enjoys feeding her family. Days like this can seem endless, but keep in mind that if your child is growing, he or she is likely getting enough nutritional value from food for proper growth and development.

Parents occasionally worry because their children choose small quantities of food and don't seem to be eating enough. Parents could learn a lot from children in this respect. Children stop eating when they are full, which is not a habit that most adults cultivate. Let your children control the amount they eat of the nutritious foods you offer them. Do not force or bribe your children to eat. Do not punish your children if they don't eat. This will only cause additional problems in the future. Let mealtime be family time, and you will feel less frustrated.

QUICK BITE

The parents' responsibility is to offer their child nutritious foods; their child's responsibility is to eat.

If your child is not eating, you must consider other factors that may cause this. Your child may be rejecting certain foods that are difficult to chew, if your child is teething, has a loose tooth, or wears braces on his or her teeth. Maybe the food is not appealing because of its smell or color. Sometimes you need to be more observant to see what is causing the problem. Don't always wait for your child to tell you.

5

Meal Solutions for Busy Families

The thought of putting together a family meal can be very stressful for many people, but it doesn't have to be that way. We're here to show you how easy it can be. Our simple solutions guide you toward bringing your family together while providing them with a healthful meal.

No Time for Breakfast

Ideally, we would all love to have extra time in the mornings. Extra time to wake up and feel refreshed, extra time to get ready, and extra time to prepare a hot, nourishing breakfast. Today's lifestyles just don't allow us this luxury.

Even though mornings in many households are rushed, there is still no excuse not to eat breakfast. Breakfast is, as we have all heard, the most important meal of the day. We break the fast from the night before, which sometimes encompasses ten hours or more since the last meal. Eating to nourish and energize the body is so important in the morning.

Many children grow up without understanding the benefits of a good breakfast, most likely because their parents—their role models—are not breakfast eaters. This can lead to a vicious cycle that creates undesirable eating habits. Everyone should realize the importance of this meal and should learn to eat something, regardless of rushed schedules and lack of prep time.

QUICK BITE

Set expectations for your family to eat breakfast every morning—and set an example, too. Your children will follow your lead.

Repeated studies have shown that children who eat breakfast perform better in school than do those who eat nothing. Many children don't get another chance to eat until noon, and that's a long time to go without nourishment. In the case of adults, lack of breakfast often increases mid-morning snacking, which may include higher-fat foods like doughnuts, sweet rolls, and so on. Do yourself a favor and try to get the whole household back on track. Seek out breakfast options that are quick, nourishing, and enjoyed by everyone in your family. Try some of the following quick and easy breakfast solutions.

- Toast or zap it. Buy breads, bagels, English muffins, frozen pancakes, waffles, or French toast that can easily be heated or toasted and eaten. When purchasing bagels or muffins, pack away a few in the freezer for busy mornings. Then eat them

QUICK BITE

Preslice bagels and freeze them. Grab a slice or two, and toast them for breakfast.

  with jam or fruit spread or cream cheese, top one with a hard-boiled egg, or spread on some hummus for a treat.

- There's always cereal. Keep a selection of whole-grain dry cereals on hand for quick breakfasts before school or work. There are so many options to choose from. If your children are set on higher-sugar options, combine their favorite with one that is lower in sugar, so that everyone is happy. Adding low-fat milk, a piece of fruit, or a small glass of juice on the side is all you need to make it through your morning.

- Add hot water or milk to instant hot cereal and zap it in the microwave. In just a few minutes, you'll have a hot, refreshing cereal, especially worth the effort on a cool morning.

- Make to-go. Pack some granola, dry cereal, and dried fruit combos in resealable bags for a quick breakfast on the run. Individual-sized cereal boxes also make great to-go options.

> **QUICK BITE**
> Keep fresh fruit like orange wedges, bananas, and grapes available to grab in a rush.

- Try a leftover. Last night's leftover chicken leg or pizza slice is another wise choice. Who made the rule that breakfast foods are the only option for breakfast?

> **QUICK BITE**
> Keep some hard-boiled eggs in your refrigerator. They make a great breakfast on the run.

- Drink a beverage for breakfast. Make a fruit shake or a smoothie. Whip it up and sip it while you're getting dressed or sending the kids out the door. You can also pour some into beverage bottles and let your kids drink it on the bus while you drink yours in the car on the way to work.

Eating on the Run

Eating out and on the run have become more common in recent years than has eating at home. With time constraints and busy schedules, it's no wonder that we eat so many meals away from home. In the future, this trend will only grow stronger.

For years, concerns and questions have arisen around the controversial issues of obesity and diets lacking balanced nutrition in the United States. Do all of these meals eaten away from home contribute to our problems? Yes, greater portion sizes are offered in many restaurants, along with an increased selection of higher-fat foods. We also see less fruits, vegetables, and whole grains eaten away from home. But on the other hand, there are more

> **QUICK BITE**
> Our poor eating habits cannot be blamed on restaurants but are a result of our own personal choices.

types of healthful, well-balanced, ready-to-go meals available at the grocery store. Many restaurants, fast-food chains, and takeout alternatives offer lower-fat sandwich wraps, salads, and child-size portions, which are available to adults as well. We can't always blame the restaurant industry for our eating problems. We are primarily responsible for what we select and consume and for what we feed our children.

Eating Out and About

Eating out refers to any experience of eating away from the home. Everything from dinner in a fancy restaurant to eating in the car falls into this category.

Sometimes we wonder whether anyone eats (or cooks) at home anymore. According to the National Restaurant Association, reports indicate that Americans (older than eight years of age) eat more than four meals out on an average week, spending upward of 60 percent of a household's total food budget to cover this extravagance. These statistics are based on the nation's many two-income families. Whenever working moms are responsible for meal preparation, they often find it easier to grab dinner on the run rather than take time to cook a meal

QUICK BITE

Whenever you eat with your family at a restaurant, a fast-food establishment, or at home, you are still a role model.

or plan ahead for meal preparation. Sometimes they feel entitled to have someone else prepare their meals because they are making extra money and have less time.

Years ago, eating out was a treat, a special occasion, a time away from the same old routine, and people thoroughly enjoyed

QUICK BITE

It's no surprise that when they were asked, many kids said they'd prefer having dinner at home with their families around the dinner table rather than fast food in the backseat of the car.

the break. Today, eating out has become second nature to many people. It is a habit and often is an effort that no one enjoys at all.

Over the last few years, reports indicate that we may be seeing a slight trend reversal regarding eating out. Apparently, more families really do want to eat at home again. Working families haven't discovered any extra time in their days, but they've found that eating out has led to spending excessive amounts of money, eating less healthfully, and raising kids who spend less time with their families. On top of all these reasons, food manufacturers are trying to make it faster and easier for parents to prepare meals at home.

Adults in the United States are concerned about health and the health of their children, particularly with the rise of obesity. Studies also indicate the importance of family members eating together to build better relationships

Occasions do arise, though, when eating away from home becomes necessary. When these times occur, be smart with your choices.

Eating well when eating out solutions

- Seek variety—Look for restaurants that offer meals that include fruits, vegetables, salads, side dishes, and whole-grain breads (even popular fast-food establishments currently meet this need).

- Watch portion sizes—Back in the 1950s, a hamburger weighed about 1.5 ounces; today, some extra-large burgers push the scale upward of 8 ounces. Look at a plate of pasta in some restaurants; one serving may be enough to feed an entire family of

QUICK BITE
Don't give in when eating out.

four. In a case like this, ask for a take-home container and save some for another meal.

- Stick with veggies—Whether on your pizza or pasta or topping your sandwich, adding vegetables to any meal is a smart choice.

- The plainer the better—Sandwiches and salads, even a baked potato, should always be ordered plain, with extras on the side. Mayonnaise, salad dressings, butter, and other sauces are best added to taste, rather than in overabundance.

- Don't give in to the breadbasket—oftentimes, the breadbasket is placed on the table when we're first seated. It's temping and easy to grab a roll or two while sipping a beverage or waiting for the meal. Try to limit the number of servings that you and your children consume. If it's too tempting, just ask that the basket be removed entirely.

QUICK BITE

Make good nutrition convenient for everyone. Stock your kitchen with many on-the-go options, such as baggies filled with trail mixes, cereal, and dried fruit, cut-up fresh vegetables, grapes, and so on. Then there is no excuse for not having a nutritious snack to take along when you're rushed.

Lunchtime

It's lunchtime and we are strapped for time! What are our choices—a few snacks at the desk or a quick lunch on the run? Or how about lunch at school or a nice casual lunch with our preschool kids at home? Too many times, lunch is not planned; it just happens somewhere around noon. "What sounds good for lunch?" is a common question both at home and away. Lunch is a time to take a midday break, refuel our bodies, and get energy to carry us through until dinnertime. Lunch should not consist of whatever we can grab, thus leaving us hungry again in a few hours and looking for more. We need to select foods that satisfy hunger and give lasting satisfaction, not just provide a quick fix.

You have many choices for a good lunch. Everyone has a different lifestyle; you need to determine what works best for you. Whether you are able to have lunch at home or you need to eat on the road or at work, you can still enjoy a tasty, nutritious, and satisfying meal.

Typically, a good lunch for a child—and for an adult, too— should include a high-protein food; a starch; fruit, a vegetable, or

QUICK BITE

If you like the idea of stashing tasty treats in your car's cup holder but hate to waste money on prepackaged convenience items from the grocery store, make your own snacks and keep them available to take with you every day.

both; a snack or a treat; and a beverage. Plan portion sizes to match the age and the size of your child. Variety is key in offering a selection of well-balanced foods that children will enjoy. Think color, texture, and flavor, too. All bland-tasting foods aren't fun; neither is an entire lunch that requires chewing. Combine soft foods, such as a turkey sandwich on a mini-bagel, with crunchy foods like baby carrots, and something sweet—say, an applesauce cup—along with low-fat milk.

With the emphasis on including more fruits and vegetables in our diets, the food industry has taken the lead to help us with our fast-paced lives. The number of grab-and-go food choices has multiplied with consumer demand. Produce companies have put fresh fruits into individual fun packages to entice children, and vegetables such as carrots and celery now can fit right into your car's cup holders. Not only are these items handy for snacks, but they're good choices when eating on the run.

Planning Your Lunch

- Again, it helps to have a general plan. With a plan, you can maintain a well-stocked pantry, refrigerator, or freezer and can thus make good choices.

QUICK BITE

Pack school and work lunches when you put dinner leftovers away; for example, use dinner rolls for sandwiches, and pack cole slaw as side dishes.

- Pack dinner leftovers into small microwavable containers so that you can reheat them when a microwave is available. For example, if a small portion of chicken and rice is left over, pack it in a container that you can take to work, or if you have left-over roast beef, put it on a roll for lunch the next day. Extra tossed salad from last night's dinner also works well for the next day's lunch.

QUICK BITE

Pack a thermos with hot soup, stew, or chili for a hearty, nutritious lunch.

- Create grab-and-go packages that contain soups, pasta dishes, stews, and other foods. You can also purchase these heat-and-eat products at the grocery store, but keep in mind that many are more costly and may also be higher in sodium or fat than you prefer. Read the nutrition labels, and use prepared convenience items in moderation.

QUICK BITE

Brown bagging is not only a term used to describe kids taking their lunches to school. Many adults are also jumping on the bandwagon and packing healthful, nutritious lunches to take to work.

Benefits of brown bagging

- Saves money. Spending on average $5 to $10 per day for lunch can add up to more than $1,000 to $2,000 each year.
- Saves time. Trying to figure out where to eat and then standing in line or waiting to be served wastes time.
- Offers greater variety. Packing your own lunch allows you to eat what you like from a variety of food choices that meet your needs.
- Controls portions. You are in charge of how much you eat. People tend to eat larger portions in restaurants in order to avoid wasting food.

Let the entire family help to make decisions about lunch, whether it's a weekend meal at home, what to purchase at the grocery store, or what to pack in a child's lunch box. If members of your family enjoy their foods, they will tend to eat better overall.

QUICK BITE

Keep several juice boxes or water bottles in your freezer to add to your child's lunch box. They make great ice packs that will defrost by lunchtime for your child to drink.

Take your kids to the grocery store with you. Ask them what they would like for lunch and find out what other kids are eating. Children who help to plan and prepare meals will enjoy them more and eat more of them. A child who is proud to open his lunch box in front of his friends will eat better.

QUICK BITE

Involve children in family food decisions. Starting with brown-bag lunches can be a great way to teach kids to make lists, keep staples on hand, and pack lunches.

Quick Lunch Solutions

Don't be afraid to try new foods. Lunches aren't all about a sandwich and potato chips anymore. Seek out new recipe ideas, such as those found later in this book, or try some of our lunchtime solutions.

- Wraps. Use tortillas or flatbread; top, spread, wrap, and roll them. You'll love everything you can make with them. Try a flavored cream cheese or mayonnaise with deli meat; hummus spread with cucumbers, peppers, onions, and lettuce; even grilled chicken with Caesar dressing and Parmesan cheese.

- Stuff. Stuffing pita bread with tuna, egg, or chicken salad can be a fun and tasty change of pace.

- Sandwich creations. Don't resort to the old familiar sandwich on white bread. Add some creativity. Use a variety of breads, such as bagels, English muffins, raisin bread, onion rolls, or even last night's leftover dinner rolls, topped with rotisserie chicken, flank steak, deli meats, peanut butter, cheeses, lettuce, tomato, and flavored mayonnaise, mustard, or salad dressing for a new twist.

- Salads. Find plastic containers that are suitable for taking lettuce on the go. Some even have small containers for salad dressing. Add toppings such as croutons, slivered almonds, dried cranberries, sunflower seeds, garbanzo beans, or even last night's leftover chicken or roast beef.

QUICK BITE

Pack fresh cut-up vegetables in plastic bags to easily grab and take on the go.

- Salads beyond lettuce. Pasta salads, fruit salads, rice salads, chicken salads, tuna salads, egg salads—they all make great choices and can be served on breads, crackers, rolls, and bagels, or even be eaten plain.

- Reheated entrees. Having access to a refrigerator and a microwave in the workplace makes it so easy to pack a meal and reheat it. Soups, stews, pasta, chili, lasagna, baked chicken—the list is endless. For kids, pack soups, chili, and stews in a wide-mouth thermos that keeps foods hot until lunchtime.

Packing lunches for yourself and your family can become part of your daily routine. Again, it may take some planning but will be well worth the effort.

Meals in Minutes

Keep a collection of surefire recipes and meal ideas available for the busiest of days. These will help you put together a meal quickly. Some favorite old standbys are already stored in the back of your mind, and you can whip them up almost from memory, without referring to the recipes at all.

Start with a collection of five or so dishes that your family loves, then add a few more along the way. No matter how busy or tired you are, you can always rely on these crowd-pleasers to make meals that your family will enjoy.

Whether you use them for an impromptu lunch when your daughter brings over a group of friends on the way to soccer practice or as a fast dinner plan because you got stuck in traffic and have only fifteen minutes to feed your family before band practice, don't despair! They will always be available. Ingredients for several of these dishes should always be stashed in your pantry, refrigerator, or freezer.

Here are a few of our favorite meals in minutes . . .

- Sandwiches and roll-ups: deli meats, cheese, or tuna fish with tortillas, flat bread, or whole-grain breads.

- Stuffed potatoes: keep potatoes stored in the pantry and stuff them with cheese, tuna fish, salsa, sour cream, or frozen spinach.

- Stir-fries: any fresh or frozen mixed vegetables, served over rice or pasta, with grated cheese. You could also add leftover cooked chicken, if desired.

- Melts: bagels and English muffins topped with leftover burgers or tuna fish, and cheese.

- Pita pockets: stuff leftovers, meats, vegetables, and even salads into a pita pocket.

- Soups: whether homemade, frozen, canned, or packaged, these make great choices on cool days.

- Panini: take out the indoor grill, grab some sourdough or another bread of choice, top it with last night's leftover cooked chicken breast, add some guacamole and salsa, and heat it.

- Eggs: eggs should always be on hand for the fastest and easiest of meals. Scrambled eggs, omelets, French toast, German pancakes—you can't get much easier than this.

- Toasted subs: another popular family favorite, just like the sandwich that takeouts serve. Some good sandwich combinations include roast beef and cheese or chicken and barbecue sauce. Top your hoagie roll, heat it, and eat it.

- Pizza: make your own pizza with prepared pizza crust or refrigerated pizza dough, pasta sauce, and shredded cheese. These are real family pleasers.

On-Hand Dinners

How many times have you stared into the pantry or the refrigerator at five o'clock trying to decide what's for dinner? In today's busy world, it happens more often than not. To combat the problem, many families eat out, carry in, or just wing it with whatever they can pull together in a flash.

Dinner doesn't have to be like this. Taking a few extra minutes to plan may be all you need to get your act together. As we said before, "Take time to maximize time."

On-Hand Dinner Solutions

Keeping the right foods available at all times will help you pull off that quick last-minute dinner without any worries. Here are some of our solutions.

- Choose pasta. Pasta can always be available, if not fresh, then in dried forms. Keep different shapes, sizes, and flavors on hand, especially the many whole-grain varieties. Pasta takes just minutes to cook and can be combined with leftovers (such as chicken, beef, or salmon) and vegetables (fresh, frozen, or canned) and topped with Parmesan cheese even on the busiest of days. Toss some noodles with oil, seasonings, and cherry tomatoes; opt for a mixture of peppers, zucchini, onions, and pesto; or create your own concoction using various sauces, including marinara, Alfredo, or vodka sauce, or homemade, if you prefer. You can make homemade pasta sauce ahead of time and freeze it. Just reheat it and pour over cooked pasta for a fast meal. Serve it with a

QUICK BITE

Keep sliced chicken and beef or other meats in your freezer for a quick and easy stir-fry. Preportion them into freezer bags, and grab them when needed.

tossed salad and some dinner rolls or crusty French bread, and you're done.

- Stir it up. Stir-fries are quick solutions to making a one-dish meal. Start with thin slices of chicken, beef, or even fresh or frozen shrimp; add cut veggies (broccoli, peppers, onions, pea pods) and flavoring, such as stir-fry sauce or teriyaki sauce. Serve it on rice, preferably brown rice, and it's ready to eat.

- Comfort foods on demand. If you enjoy the comforts of a steaming hot meal or maybe a hearty meat-and-potato combination, try these tips. Keep individually packed, boneless, skinless chicken breasts on hand or even individually packed fish fillets. Why not include some chops or steaks that you wrapped up separately, too? Pop the meat into a twenty- or thirty-minute jarred marinade or top it with your own choice (such as teriyaki sauce, barbecue sauce, a seasoned rub, or just salt and pepper). Bake, broil, or grill your meat—it will take fewer than thirty minutes. Add a side of baked potatoes (white or sweet) that you microwave for five minutes, place some fresh fruit (such as a melon slice or strawberries) or fresh veggies (sugar snap peas) on the plate, and dinner's ready.

- Pack ready-to-eat pouches. Tuna, salmon, and cooked chicken in every flavor, including lemon-pepper, sweet and spicy, garlic, and plain, work great on a sandwich, in a salad, on top of pasta, or, best yet, right out of the pouch. These pouches require no refrigeration (until opened) and offer a wide range of choices.

- Got soup? Soup has become one of the fastest and most popular foods today. Nourishing and comforting, as well as filling, soups appeal to people of all ages. There are so many varieties, too. Make at home on the weekend and freeze individual portions, or keep canned soup or quick soup mixes on hand for a hearty soup in a flash. Add some cornbread, biscuits, crackers, or hot rolls, and this quick meal will meet your needs on a cool (or warm) evening. Pour hot soup into a thermos for those cool days when you're on the go. Sip it in the car or while you watch a soccer game in the park.

QUICK BITE

Double the recipes for soups and stews when you make them. Pack up the extra amounts and freeze them. They will come in handy on another day.

- Grilling can be done year round, in all weather conditions and all locations. If you don't have a backyard grill, purchase a small indoor variety. No longer does the weather have to be ideal to heat up the grill. Use your choice of marinated meat as mentioned previously or maybe a burger, a veggie burger, or a salmon fillet; add fresh steamed vegetables, a prepared garlic loaf, and fresh pineapple, if you like. What a great meal!

- There's always breakfast. Those quick-and-easy grabs for breakfast can also be handy on extremely busy evenings. There's nothing wrong with making scrambled eggs with cheese, an omelet with fresh (or leftover) vegetables or meats, and serving bagels on the side. Frittatas make good quick choices, as well as French toast, pancakes, German pancakes, and waffles. Top them with fruit spread or fresh fruit, serve glasses of milk, and everyone's happy. And for those really crazy days, there's always cereal. Kids get a real kick out of this.

- Make your own takeout. Common takeout foods include pizza and Chinese and Mexican foods. Why not try to make your own? It doesn't take a lot of time or energy to come up

QUICK BITE

Any type of food can fit into a healthful diet. Just be sure to balance the food choices within each meal. *Variety*, *balance*, and *moderation* are the key words to remember.

with some quick solutions for pizza (such as pizza bagels or French bread pizza), Chinese food (egg rolls or sweet and sour chicken), Mexican foods (taco bar), or even to build your own sub sandwich. Families love these meals.

Create a Cycle Menu

A cycle menu for home use is a valuable guide for meal planning. Hang the menu inside your pantry door for quick reference. You can create a weekly, a biweekly, or a monthly menu. Base it on new foods to try or old family favorites, or you can even identify each night of the week (Sunday—chicken night; Monday—burger night; Tuesday—breakfast night) according to a theme. Whatever works for you! This cycle menu allows you to think ahead, plan ahead, shop ahead, and know immediately what is planned each night. It also lets the family join in and help whenever possible.

Following is a two-week sample dinner menu we created to help you get started.

WHAT'S FOR DINNER TONIGHT?

Week 1

Sunday	Monday	Tuesday	Wednesday
Company Chicken*	Turkey Chili*	cheese omelet	Flounder Parmesan*
Orange Glazed Carrots*	dinner rolls	whole wheat bagel	Mashed Potatoes (or Not)*
hot cooked pasta	fresh fruit salad	cantaloupe wedge	Dilled Green Beans*

Thursday	Friday	Saturday
Creamy Tomato Soup*	leftovers	Ravioli Lasagna*
Mini Pizza Bagels*		steamed broccoli
mandarin oranges		garlic toast

Week 2

Sunday	Monday	Tuesday	Wednesday
Sweet and Sour Glazed Chicken* Oriental Spinach* breadsticks	veggie burgers tomato/lettuce salad whole-grain buns	Quick Vegetable Frittata* Cheese Biscuits* strawberry slices	Southwestern Salmon* wild rice Dilled Green Beans*

Thursday	Friday	Saturday
Mom's Potato Soup* Grilled Cheese Sandwich* carrot/celery sticks	leftovers	Tuna Noodle Casserole* tossed green salad assorted grapes

Indicates that a recipe is included in this book.

Fast Favorites

We're all looking for "fast foods." Not necessarily the ones served in fast-food restaurants, but foods that can be prepared fast. Food manufacturers see this need and present more options to us every year.

Look at some of the prepackaged meals now offered at your local grocery store. There are frozen options (ready-to-eat and heat-and-eat), packaged options (add a meat to a prepared rice or pasta, and you're good to go), and fresh options (containing fresh meat and vegetables already cut up and ready to cook). Look for these products all over the supermarket. Food manufacturers will do whatever it takes to draw us to their products and enable us to save our precious time.

Are Frozen Dinners Good Choices?

This $6 billion industry has surely taken off in recent years, but are these good options for a fast meal? Years ago, when TV dinners were first introduced, the choices were very limited, but they did give mothers a reprieve from the daily cooking routine. Just grabbing a TV tray and heating up your meal was a novelty and a treat for the family. Kids loved them, and moms loved the break.

We now see a surge of microwavable heat-and-eat meals, skillet and oven meal kits, Crock Pot or slow-cooker meals, kid-friendly frozen meals, low-fat meals, and so many more. In fact, the collection of frozen meals takes up almost an entire aisle at the grocery store.

If you are concerned about the nutritional value of these dinners, you can rest assured that these meals are in fact fine, if eaten in moderation. This means once in a while, maybe once or twice a week. Freezers, containers, and techniques have greatly improved, which has enhanced the quality of the frozen foods or dishes. Many frozen food manufacturers are making it easier for everyone by offering choices that include low-fat and low-calorie varieties. They want families to realize that these meals, packaged to be taken home and shared among family members, are actually a better option than going to a drive-through. At least children will learn the value of eating at home and being with their families around the dinner table.

A great benefit to frozen meals is portion control. Some people may think the portions look a little skimpy when they open the boxes, but in most cases the portions are in range or are adequate in size. So for anyone attempting weight control, this built-in portion control may be a good thing.

Educated consumers want to know what they are buying, how they are spending their money, and what value they are getting. Consumers must read the labels of the various products and make sure the specific foods are in line with their needs. If the expense of prepackaged frozen foods seems a little too high for your budget, figure out how you can prepare your own frozen meals. This will allow you to focus on family favorites, preportion accordingly, and know the quality and the value of the meals you serve. With a little advance planning, you can make nutritious frozen dinners quickly and without breaking your budget, and you can stock your freezer with them.

Pick the best (or worst) frozen meal

- Choose thin-crust pizzas or red marinara sauce instead of thick or stuffed crust pizzas and creamy white sauces on pastas.

- Opt for dinners with no more than 300 to 400 calories per meal. This way, you can add a salad, some low-fat milk, or frozen yogurt for dessert and still fall into a good dinner range for calories.

QUICK BITE

A convenience food is a food that can easily be prepared for consumption.

- Check out the saturated fat. Select products that have no more than 6 to 7 grams of saturated fat, which is about one third of your daily needs.

- Look for sodium levels to stay below 600 milligrams.

- And, most important, eat prepared frozen meals in moderation. Don't make them a staple in your diet.

Packaged Convenience Foods

Convenience is expensive. Purchasing any convenience food will cost more than if you buy old-fashioned, plain, and simple foods, but the trend toward offering more convenience products is widespread. It's what people want today. In fact, so many packaged, microwavable convenience foods are available now, that many young children will likely grow up not knowing how to use a traditional oven.

Supermarkets react to consumer demand. Customers tend to prefer prepackaged produce over unwrapped fresh produce. Look around your local store and notice the abundance of fresh produce packed in high-tech plastic bags, some of it even prewashed and precut. Often, these bags allow the produce to last longer than its alternative, but always remember to check the "sell-by" date. Yes, we pay more for produce that is already washed and cut into bite-size pieces, but it's what we want.

QUICK BITE

Convenience is no longer a luxury but is something that consumers expect.

Benefits of convenience foods

- Convenience foods reduce the time it takes to prepare meals.
- Convenience foods offer a wide variety of choices, whether packaged, canned, or frozen. Many seasonal foods are available year-round.
- Food safety is less of a concern because high-tech packaging and processing techniques allow for minimal spoilage and fewer bacteria than in fresh alternatives.
- Many convenience foods have a greater shelf life, sometimes up to six months.

Along with the produce, check out other convenience foods in your grocery store. There are now packaged and fresh items in the dairy and meat departments, ranging from pudding cups to kid-size lunch box snacks to already-cooked Buffalo chicken wings, potato salad, and party hors d'oeuvres trays. You can find convenience foods almost anywhere in the store. Many times, these items are even shelved together to help you find everything you need in one place.

Not all convenience foods are created equal. Learn to read labels to determine exactly what the foods contain. Choose high-fat and high-sodium products in moderation. Educate yourself on healthful convenience options. It will benefit your family in the long run.

Based on household needs, every individual should determine which products work best for his or her family. If saving time in food preparation is your priority and the expense is secondary, then by all means use them. If you can find better alternatives, then do so. Just remember that your main goal is feeding yourself and your family at home as healthfully as possible. Make sure that whatever path you take allows you to do so.

Cook Now, Save Some for Later

Planning ahead can make mealtime so much easier and less chaotic. Cooking now and saving some for later is a great timesaver, allowing us to have variety and tasty meals despite our hectic lives.

Many recipes in this book can be prepared ahead of time and frozen. Some people are afraid of the freezer, not being certain what should and should not be frozen. We will offer some helpful suggestions.

First, as we said, think ahead. Depending on your schedule, it's probably difficult to prepare dinner each and every night. Yet with a little preplanning, you can prepare for hectic nights ahead. For example, if you are making a chicken or beef dish, make one or two portions extra. It won't take any extra time, and you'll be assured of some extra to freeze. You may want to make shredded fajitas or chili later in the week or month. This cooked chicken or beef can come in handy for a quick, throw-together meal. Preparing double or even triple the amount and freezing some helps you to have foods on standby.

QUICK BITE

When cooking chicken breasts, always make one or two extra that you can toss in salads or slice for a sandwich.

Freezing portions in individual containers will keep foods available for all members of the family. You can grab one or two (or more) portions on demand and heat them as necessary. Freezing individual portions may also be possible if adequate amounts are left over from a meal.

Benefits of freezing precooked meals

- You can prepare meals at your convenience.
- These meals are more healthful than store-bought options.
- The meals are more economical.
- The meals can be planned to include your family's favorite foods.

When precooking and freezing, keep these tips in mind:

- Foods will require reheating before you serve them. When preparing meals specifically for reheating and serving at another time, plan to slightly undercook them.
- Cool precooked meals before portioning and placing them into the freezer. Hot foods placed into the freezer can cause

changes in freezer temperatures and can also affect the quality and the taste of the food.

- Wrap preportioned meals properly using freezer wraps, bags, and airtight containers designed for freezing. This will allow for adequate freezing, ensure the quality of the food, and will help to prevent odors and leaks. Leave as little air as possible in bags and freezer containers, but leave enough to allow room for expansion, which can occur.

- Place preportioned, cooked meal portions into the coolest part of the freezer for quick, complete freezing.

QUICK BITE

Think, cook once . . . eat twice or three times. Make a roasted chicken on the weekend, and then use leftover chicken in tacos, fajitas, sandwiches, and salads throughout the week.

The Best Use of Your Precooked Freezer Meals

Even though freezer meals can last a long time, be smart with how long you actually keep them frozen. Follow this chart as a guide for freezing precooked meals.

Freezing Guide for Precooked Foods

Precooked Food	How Long to Freeze
beef	3–4 months
chicken/poultry	up to 1 month
in gravy/sauce	3–4 months
casseroles	2–3 months
soups	up to 3 months
cooked pasta/lasagna	2–3 months
vegetables in sauce	up to 6 months

You need to be the judge of the food's quality after it has been frozen. If the food doesn't look or smell good, discard it. If you are in any way doubtful of its use, throw it out. Food that thaws due to freezer malfunction should be cooked and eaten. Do not refreeze thawed foods.

QUICK BITE

When packing precooked foods or leftovers for the freezer, allow warm foods to cool down properly for faster freezing.

When preparing casseroles, look at the amounts needed in the recipe. For example, you may not need a whole chicken or you may have cooked extra pieces. With a little preplanning, the amount that isn't needed may be stored and used in a different recipe. This time-saving idea is often called "cook once and eat twice."

How to cook once and eat twice

- Prepare a rotisserie chicken for one meal, and save some cooked chicken to shred for BBQ chicken sandwiches or to add to a chicken Caesar salad tomorrow.

- Prepare ground beef to make meat sauce for spaghetti, and save some cooked ground beef for tacos during the week.

- Grill a flank steak on Sunday night for dinner, and reserve half to make fajitas on Tuesday.

- Prepare our Creamy Mac and Cheese for one night and make one of the 3-Way variations to carry through another night.

QUICK BITE

A typical two-and-a-half-pound (cooked) rotisserie chicken will yield approximately four cups of meat, which is plenty to serve to a family of four.

QUICK BITE

Keep a variety of frozen fruits and vegetables on hand for days when fresh produce is not available.

The freezer can be a good friend to busy people. We all know it's not possible to prepare a home-cooked meal completely or partially from scratch night after night. But by thinking ahead, you can prepare many meals in advance and use your freezer to keep them for another day.

Take Time to Feed Your Freezer

Sometimes our busy schedules lead to an increased consumption of not-so-nutritious, unbalanced meals. Most people don't realize that their home freezers could be the solution to this problem. Relying on your freezer could offer you a new world of more healthful food choices. Try freezing individually packed raw foods that can be easily defrosted and cooked, freezing leftovers, freezing precooked foods, and freezing small portions of ready-to-cook foods.

QUICK BITE

Purchase large-sized packages of chicken or other meat (on sale, if possible) to divide up, wrap in small batches, and defrost when needed. Note that after the meat is frozen and thawed, it must be cooked. It cannot be refrozen raw, but it can be frozen after it is cooked.

The next time you prepare dinner, make an extra serving of pasta sauce, soup, chili, pancakes, or lasagna. These all heat up beautifully after being frozen. When purchasing ground meat (beef or turkey), chicken breasts, and fish fillets, separate the contents of large packages, and freeze everything in small portions for easy defrosting.

Wrapping foods properly should be a primary concern. You want the foods that you put into your freezer to come out as fresh and tasty as they were originally. Make sure that you use top-quality wraps, bags, and containers. Freezer burn results from dehydration of food that was not properly packed. If you're packing away leftovers, wrap them tightly and label them with the type of food and the date. Keeping track of food in the freezer ensures that they will be used in a timely manner.

Remember that thawing your frozen food is just as important as freezing it. Frozen foods should not be thawed at room temperature because it can jeopardize the safety of the food. The best ways to thaw include:

- Refrigerate the food overnight to slowly raise the temperature of the food without compromising its safety.

- Use the microwave on the defrost cycle. Refer to the manufacturer's guide for specific details and timing.

- Place the wrapped frozen food in cool water that is changed every 30 minutes.

The best use of your freezer

- Pack food into individual servings. (This allows food to freeze and be reheated more quickly.)

- Let leftovers and cooked foods cool to room temperature before placing them in the freezer. Putting foods that are too hot into the freezer can affect the quality and the taste of the food.

- Use appropriate freezer containers, wraps, and freezer bags.

- Once meat is already thawed, it must be cooked. It cannot be refrozen raw, but it can be frozen after it is cooked.

- Visit farmers' markets in the summertime, and purchase berries to freeze for the cooler months. You'll be glad to have them on hand for cobblers, dessert toppings, smoothies, or muffins.

QUICK BITE

If you're not sure whether to freeze a particular food, try it with a small portion and see how it tastes after being thawed and reheated.

What's Good to Freeze (Raw/Fresh)*

Food	How Long
breads/muffins/bagels	2–3 months
cakes/pies/cookies	3–6 months
cookie dough	up to 3 months
butter	up to 9 months
vegetables in a sauce	up to 6 months
fruits (bananas/berries)	up to 2 months
sauces	up to 3 months
chicken	up to 6 months
luncheon meats/hot dogs	1–2 months
fish	up to 3 months

This is just a guide. Your personal experience with your freezer will indicate what works best for you and your family.

What Doesn't Freeze Well at Home*

- vegetables and fruits with a high concentration of water, such as lettuce, whole tomatoes, celery, and watermelon
- cooked egg whites/yolks or icings made with egg whites
- whole eggs in shell/raw or cooked
- raw potatoes
- plain cooked pasta/rice without sauce
- mayonnaise/sour cream/cream cheese/cottagecheese/ricotta cheese
- cream/custard pies/desserts with cream, meringue, or custard fillings
- gelatin
- soups or stews thickened with cornstarch or flour
- thickened sauces
- fried/battered home-cooked foods

Commercial freezers are different from home freezers. Although you shouldn't freeze these foods at home, you will sometimes see these products available in grocery store freezers.

Once each month (that's only twelve times in the year), spend a little time making freezer meals. Visit a local warehouse club

QUICK BITE

Freezer burn is actually dehydration of the food that destroys the cell structure and ruins the food's flavor, texture, and quality. Proper freezer storage can eliminate this problem.

that allows you to buy foods in bulk (and at a good price), and cook a variety of meals from these ingredients. Then, stock up your freezer. On your busiest days during the rest of the month, pull out your dated and labeled food packages, and you can prepare dinner in minutes.

New franchises and businesses are jumping on this bandwagon. Many different store-front businesses now bring together groups of people, particularly moms, to collectively prepare two and three weeks of meals in one afternoon, which are then taken home and frozen. Not only is the gathering fun and social, but the response is positive, indicating that many people like the convenience of having tasty, healthful meals ready to eat.

One-Dish Dinners

Wouldn't it be great to come home every night to a hot cooked meal? Even if dinner isn't waiting on the table for you and your family, wouldn't it be nice to at least have it prepared and ready to heat and eat?

One-dish dinners are all about combining your meat, vegetables, and potatoes or another starch, together in one dish. You can serve this with a side salad or some fruit and have a complete meal. One-dish dinners are popular with families, whether they're prepared in the oven or slow-cooked all day in a crockpot or a similar cooker.

There's nothing better than having a hot meal after a long day, but most of us probably don't have this luxury. Maybe we don't have time to prepare complicated meals or don't want to create stacks of dirty dishes. Yet we still prefer home-cooked meals over fast food, microwavable convenience dinners, or cold sandwiches.

The good news is that you can have what you desire, and it's all in one dish. We're going to teach you how to plan one-dish dinners for those long, crazy days when you arrive home at six o'clock with no other options.

QUICK BITE

Check out the simplified slow-cooker meals that are available in your grocery store. You can even buy throwaway liners to keep cleanup to a minimum. Dinner doesn't get much easier than this.

One-Dish Meal Solutions

Think stir-fries, casseroles, skillet meals, pasta, or soup. All of these options can come together in thirty minutes or less, without a lot of thought. Keeping staples on hand and planning ahead may be all you need today.

When it comes to stir-fries, anything works. Take boneless, skinless chicken breast or last night's leftover cooked chicken or maybe some beef, lean pork, salmon, or seafood. Add it to any combination of sautéed vegetables you prefer, frozen or fresh. There are frozen stir-fry vegetables already prepackaged, or you can mix together broccoli, onions, peppers, and water chestnuts. Stir in a little bottled stir-fry sauce, teriyaki sauce, chicken broth, or even soy sauce as desired.

Casseroles and baked pastas, such as ziti, are family favorites, too. Toss your pasta (uncooked) with a little water and pasta sauce, stir it up, bake it, top it with shredded mozzarella cheese, and your meal is ready. Or why not combine uncooked rice with chicken and top it with your favorite creamed soup? Cook it over the stovetop for a delicious comfort meal. Our Tuna Noodle Casserole is an old family favorite that can be made according to your family's preferences—if your children don't like peas, substitute broccoli or top it with shredded cheese for extra flavor and protein.

QUICK BITE

On days when you have time, chop up some extra vegetables, freeze them in small quantities, and use them for stir-fry dishes, soups, stews, and toppings.

Soups and stews are also wise choices. You can prepare many of them in a slow cooker if you choose, or you can find other recipes that can be whipped up quickly and easily.

One-dish dinners enable you to serve a hot meal in record time, and there are few dishes to clean. What more could you ask for?

Your Quick Meal Solution Planning Guide

Now that you have thought up some new ideas on how to feed your family with our meal solutions, it's time to create your personal planning guide. Use whatever system works best for you.

We've provided you with suggestions that include some of our new recipes and a few easy pair-ups to balance your meals healthfully and easily. A note follows each recipe, suggesting how you can balance the meal. You can either use our suggestions or find other choices that work better for you and that will please your family.

Start by planning one month at a time for your main meal of the day. Create a grid such as the one that follows, add several theme meal nights, jot down a few favorite dishes, then set your family and personal goals. You can begin by using our meal suggestions, then fill in your own favorites. Hang this chart where everyone in the family can view it. Eventually, members of your family will add to the list, and planning will become second nature to you. Once you realize how easy and practical planning can be, you'll wonder why you haven't done this before.

MEAL PLANNING CALENDAR

Weekly Planner	Sunday	Monday	Tuesday	Wednesday	Thursday	Friday	Saturday
			Chicken Night		*Family Favorite Night*		*Pasta Night*
Week 1	Organize recipe file; try one new recipe this week		Buy rotisserie chicken	Make chicken wraps for lunch from leftover chicken	Leftover fried rice		
Week 2	Clean out pantry, fill with staples	Dinner in a Dish	Chicken and Brown Rice Pilaf; Fruity Acorn Squash		Tuna Melt; Quick Tomato Rice Soup		Easy Pasta Stir-Fry
Week 3	Plan family brunch; Famous Baked Apple Pancake		Chicken Nachos; Hearty Sweet and Sour Slaw		Make tacos tonight	Soup and Sandwich Dinner	Fettuccine Broccoli Alfredo
Week 4	Prepare extra batch of Apple Raisin Muffins to freeze		Easy Baked Chicken	Make chicken salad for lunch from leftovers	Pull-Apart Pizza		Cheesy Mac and Cheese
Week 5	Prepare Our Favorite Meatloaf	Meatloaf sandwich for lunch from leftovers	Company Chicken		Steak and Pepper Fajitas, Mini Egg Rolls, Mandarin Oranges		

Family Goals

- Eat together at least three nights each week.
- Set a schedule listing who's responsible for setting the table each night and who's responsible for cleaning up.

Personal Goals

- Clean out the recipe file.
- Select and try one new recipe each week for a month.

Foods to Add to Shopping List

_____

_____

_____

_____

_____

_____

_____

6

Recipes

T he recipes in this book are just a sample of many easy-to-prepare meals you may enjoy. Every recipe you add to your collection will help you and your family to eat healthfully and enjoy your meals together. Make a habit of trying new recipes for your quick meal solutions.

The nutrient breakdown is provided by the Food Processor II Nutritional Analysis Software. Calories, protein, carbohydrates, fat, cholesterol, fiber, and calcium are indicated. Figures are rounded to the closest whole number. When several food choices are provided, the first food listed is included in the analysis. Optional ingredients are not analyzed.

The information in the analysis can help you plan meals for each day. If one meal includes a high-fat food, select a low-fat choice for other meals in the same day. It's all about balance. Be sure to put food groups that are missing from one meal into other meals of the day. For example, if your lunch doesn't include fruit or vegetables, add them to dinner or to a snack during the day.

We also gave suggestions for balancing your meal as a means to help you start planning. Foods marked with an asterisk (*) indicate that the recipe is included within our collection. If you choose to select other foods, be sure they balance accordingly.

Happy, healthful eating. Enjoy!

BREAKFASTS

Berry Banana Smoothie

A refreshing beverage helps everyone start the day off right.

> 1 cup low-fat milk
> 1 (6-ounce) container low-fat strawberry yogurt
> ¼ cup strawberries or raspberries, frozen
> 1 frozen banana, sliced

Place all of the ingredients in a blender. Blend them on high until they're smooth. Serve immediately.

Makes 2 servings.

Calories per serving: 207
Protein: 8 g
Carbohydrates: 37 g
Fat: 3 g
Cholesterol: 15 mg
Fiber: 2 g
Calcium: 249 mg

To balance your meal, add: Cheese Biscuits*, orange juice

Applesauce Smoothie

Berry-flavored applesauce works great, too.

½ cup applesauce
½ cup apple juice, chilled
1 (8-ounce) container low-fat vanilla yogurt

Place all of the ingredients in a blender. Blend until they're smooth. Serve immediately.

Makes 2 servings.

Calories per serving: 152
Protein: 6 g
Carbohydrates: 30 g
Fat: 1 g
Cholesterol: 6 mg
Fiber: 1 g
Calcium: 200 mg

To balance your meal, add: Quick Vegetable Frittata*,
orange wedges

Orange Creamsicle Smoothie

That creamsicle taste is a favorite of kids and adults alike.

1 cup low-fat milk
1 (8 ounce) container low-fat vanilla yogurt
¼ cup orange juice

Combine all of the ingredients in a blender. Blend until they're smooth. Serve immediately.

Makes 2 servings.

Calories per serving: 171
Protein: 10 g
Carbohydrates: 25 g
Fat: 4 g
Cholesterol: 15 mg
Fiber: 0
Calcium: 346 mg

To balance your meal, add: Moist Berry Muffin,
melon cubes*

Open-Faced Fruit Sandwich

Try other fresh fruit slices to suit your mood.

¼ cup low-fat cream cheese, softened
2 slices whole-grain bread, toasted
2 strawberries, sliced
1 banana, sliced

Spread the cream cheese over the toast. Top it with the sliced fruit.

Makes 2 servings.

Calories per serving: 164
Protein: 5 g
Carbohydrates: 29 g
Fat: 5 g
Cholesterol: 13 mg
Fiber: 7 g
Calcium: 131 mg

To balance your meal, add: hard- or soft-boiled egg,
low-fat milk, orange juice or fruit of choice

Moist Berry Muffins

Substitute fresh or frozen raspberries for the blueberries.

    2 cups flour
    ½ cup sugar
    1 teaspoon baking soda
    1 teaspoon baking powder
    ¼ teaspoon salt
    1 egg
    ¼ cup orange juice
    2 tablespoons vegetable oil
    1 teaspoon vanilla extract
    1 (8-ounce) container low-fat vanilla yogurt
    ¾ cup blueberries, fresh or frozen
    cooking spray

Preheat the oven to 375 degrees F.

In a large bowl, combine the flour, sugar, baking soda, baking powder, and salt. Push the dry ingredients to the outside of the bowl and add the egg, orange juice, oil, vanilla extract, and yogurt to the center. Stir them together until the ingredients are just moistened. Lightly fold in the blueberries.

Spray a muffin pan with the cooking spray. Distribute the batter evenly into the pan cups, filling them about three-quarters full. Bake them 18 to 20 minutes or until golden brown and a toothpick inserted into the muffins comes out clean.

Cool the muffins in the pan slightly before removing and serving.

Makes 1 dozen muffins.

Calories per serving: 159
Protein: 4 g
Carbohydrates: 29 g
Fat: 3 g
Cholesterol: 19 mg
Fiber: 1 g
Calcium: 61 mg

To balance your meal, add:
scrambled egg,
low-fat milk,
fruit of choice

Veggie Pita Scramble

*Use last night's leftover veggies, such as broccoli, squash, or
mixed vegetables, as a substitution for the peppers.*

> 1 tablespoon vegetable oil
> ¼ cup green pepper, chopped
> ¼ cup red pepper, chopped
> 2 eggs
> 1 pita, cut in half

In a small skillet, heat the oil. Add the peppers and sauté until tender. Add the eggs. Cook until the eggs are set.

Stuff each pita half with the scrambled egg mixture. Eat them immediately or wrap them in foil and eat them on the run.

Makes 2 servings (half a pita per serving).

Calories per serving: 178
Protein: 8 g
Carbohydrates: 20 g
Fat: 7 g
Cholesterol: 187 mg
Fiber: 1 g
Calcium: 51 mg

To balance your meal, add: fruit cup, low-fat milk

Breakfast Egg and Cheese Puffs

Kids love these puffs. They can easily be made ahead of time and reheated as desired.

cooking spray
1 (16-ounce) can biscuit dough, 8 biscuits
4 eggs, beaten
½ cup cheddar cheese, shredded

Preheat the oven to 375 degrees F. Spray a muffin pan with the cooking spray.

Divide the biscuit dough into 8 precut pieces. Press each piece into a muffin pan cup. Evenly divide the beaten eggs among the 8 cups, and top each piece of dough with about 1 tablespoon shredded cheese. Bake them 10 to 12 minutes until the puffs are golden brown.

Makes 8 breakfast puffs (1 puff per serving).

Calories per serving: 220
Protein: 10 g
Carbohydrates: 31 g
Fat: 6 g
Cholesterol: 114 mg
Fiber: 0
Calcium: 63 mg

To balance your meal, add: melon cubes, low-fat milk

Peanut Butter and Banana Sandwich

Try also making this on a bagel, an English muffin, or cinnamon raisin bread.

1 slice whole-grain bread
1 tablespoon peanut butter
1 small banana, sliced
honey, if desired

Toast the bread, if you prefer. Spread it with peanut butter. Top it with banana slices and drizzle the sandwich with honey, if desired. Fold it in half to eat it.

Makes 1 serving.

Calories per serving: 248
Protein: 7 g
Carbohydrates: 41 g
Fat: 9 g
Cholesterol: 0
Fiber: 8 g
Calcium: 112 mg

To balance your meal, add: sliced strawberries, low-fat milk

Cinnamon Toast Sticks

Take the entire bag of toast sticks along with you for a breakfast on the run.

2 slices whole-grain bread, toasted
1 tablespoon margarine or butter, melted
2 teaspoons sugar
½ teaspoon cinnamon

Cut each slice of toast into 4 strips. Brush them with melted margarine or butter. Drop the toast sticks into a resealable plastic bag. Add the sugar and cinnamon to the bag. Seal it and shake well.

Makes 2 servings.

Calories per serving: 129
Protein: 2 g
Carbohydrates: 19 g
Fat: 6 g
Cholesterol: 6 mg
Fiber: 5 g
Calcium: 107 mg

*To balance your meal, add: hard-boiled egg,
low-fat chocolate milk*

Quick Vegetable Frittata

This is a great way to use last night's leftovers for a quick breakfast.

cooking spray
¼ cup broccoli or any vegetable of choice (use last night's leftovers), chopped, cooked
2 eggs, beaten
1 tablespoon Parmesan cheese, grated

Spray a small skillet with the cooking spray. Add the broccoli and heat it until it's warm. Top it with the beaten eggs and cheese. Cover and cook for 2 minutes until it's set.

Makes 1 serving.

Calories per serving: 184
Protein: 16 g
Carbohydrates: 3 g
Fat: 12 g
Cholesterol: 430 mg
Fiber: 1 g
Calcium: 145 mg

To balance your meal, add: fresh berries, low-fat milk

Apple Streusel Bites

For a fun treat, make these in a mini-muffin pan. These mini-streusel puffs make a fun grab-and-go breakfast.

cooking spray
1 (6-ounce) can biscuit dough
2 apples, peeled and chopped
1 tablespoon sugar
½ teaspoon cinnamon

Preheat the oven to 350 degrees F.

Spray a muffin pan with the cooking spray. Divide the biscuit dough into 6 pieces. Press each piece into a muffin pan cup. Evenly divide the chopped apples onto the top of the dough.

In a small bowl, combine the sugar and cinnamon. Sprinkle this on top of the apples. Bake the puffs 10 to 12 minutes until they're golden brown.

Makes 6 streusel puffs (1 puff per serving).

Calories per serving: 103
Protein: 2 g
Carbohydrates: 23 g
Fat: 1 g
Cholesterol: 0
Fiber: 2 g
Calcium: 2 mg

To balance your meal, add: soft-boiled egg, grapefruit juice

Famous Baked Apple Pancake

On a weekend when you have more time, try this delectable treat. It's also great cold as breakfast the next day.

> 2 tablespoons margarine
> 2 small tart green apples, thinly sliced, but not peeled
> ½ low-fat milk
> ½ cup flour
> 3 eggs, beaten
> 1 teaspoon sugar
>
> *Topping:*
> ¼ cup sugar
> 1 teaspoon cinnamon

Preheat the oven to 450 degrees F.

In a large skillet, heat the margarine. Add the apples and cook until they're softened. Pour them into a 9-inch pie pan.

In a small bowl, combine the milk, flour, eggs, and 1 teaspoon of sugar. Mix these well. Pour the batter over the apples. Put the skillet into the preheated oven for 8 minutes.

Combine the topping ingredients. Sprinkle them over the pancake. Return it to the oven for an additional 7 minutes. Cut the pancake into 6 wedges. Serve it immediately.

Makes 6 servings.

Calories per serving: 149
Protein: 5 g
Carbohydrates: 17 g
Fat: 7 g
Cholesterol: 112 mg
Fiber: 2 g
Calcium: 40 mg

To balance your meal, add: melon wedge, low-fat milk

Breakfast Coffee Cake

Make this easy coffee cake on a weekend, and keep it on hand for a quick weekday breakfast as you are running out the door.

cooking spray
20 frozen white bread rolls
½ package butterscotch pudding (not instant)
⅓ cup margarine, melted
½ cup brown sugar
1 teaspoon cinnamon

Spray a large bundt or angel cake pan with the cooking spray.

Add the rolls all around the bottom. Sprinkle the pudding mix over the rolls. Combine the melted margarine with the brown sugar, and pour it over the rolls. Sprinkle the cinnamon on top. Cover the rolls with plastic wrap. Let them rise overnight.

Preheat the oven to 350 degrees F. Bake the cake 30 to 35 minutes. Serve it warm or refrigerate it and reheat it in the microwave, as desired.

Makes 12 servings.

Calories per serving: 181
Protein: 3 g
Carbohydrates: 27 g
Fat: 7 g
Cholesterol: 5 mg
Fiber: 0
Calcium: 22 mg

To balance your meal, add: sliced strawberries, low-fat milk

Cheese Biscuits

Jazz up your weekend breakfasts with a twist on an old favorite. Then save some biscuits to grab during the week.

> 2 cups buttermilk biscuit mix
> ⅔ cup low-fat milk
> ½ cup low-fat cheddar cheese, shredded
> 2 tablespoons margarine or butter, melted
> ½ teaspoon garlic powder

Preheat the oven to 450 degrees F.

Combine the biscuit mix with the milk and cheddar cheese. Stir this until a soft dough forms, then mix it vigorously for 30 seconds.

Drop the dough by heaping tablespoons onto an ungreased cookie sheet. Bake the biscuits 8 to 10 minutes, until they're golden brown.

Combine the melted margarine or butter with the garlic powder and brush this over the warm biscuits before removing them from the cookie sheet. Serve them warm.

Makes 12 biscuits (1 biscuit per serving).

Calories per serving: 118
Protein: 3 g
Carbohydrates: 13 g
Fat: 5 g
Cholesterol: 5 mg
Fiber: 0
Calcium: 72 mg

To balance your meal, add: scrambled egg, orange slices, low-fat milk

Caramel Apple Popover

This is a great weekend treat for breakfast or brunch.

4 medium tart apples: Granny Smith, Rome, Jonathan, or
 other cooking apples
2 tablespoons margarine or butter
⅔ cup brown sugar
cooking spray
1 cup flour
¾ teaspoon salt
2 large eggs
1 cup low-fat milk

Preheat the oven to 450 degrees F. Wash, peel, and core the apples. Slice the apples into ½-inch to ¾-inch pieces.

In a saucepan over low heat, melt the margarine or butter. Add the brown sugar. Stir in the apple slices and sauté until the apples are tender and glazed. Pour the mixture into a 9-by-9-inch baking dish, sprayed with the cooking spray.

Mix the flour and salt in a small mixing bowl. In another small bowl, lightly beat the eggs and milk. Slowly add the flour to the milk mixture and beat this until smooth. Pour the batter (it will be thin) over the apple slices. Bake the popover 20 minutes until the topping looks puffed (or popped) and not too brown. Reduce the oven temperature to 350 degrees F. Bake the popover 20 minutes longer or until the top is a deep golden brown. Serve it warm.

Makes 8 servings.

Calories per serving: 219
Protein: 4 g
Carbohydrates: 41 g
Fat: 5 g
Cholesterol: 58 mg
Fiber: 2 g
Calcium: 61 mg

To balance your meal, add: orange wedges, low-fat milk

Margaret's Banana Bread

This is a wonderful fruit bread, light in color and not too sweet. Bake some on the weekend, and wrap up a slice or two for a quick snack during the week.

cooking spray
2 cups flour
1 teaspoon baking powder
½ teaspoon baking soda
½ teaspoon salt
⅔ cup sugar
⅓ cup margarine or butter, softened
2 large eggs
1 cup banana (about 3 bananas), mashed
2 tablespoons lemon juice
3 tablespoons buttermilk
½ cup pecans or walnuts, chopped (optional)

Preheat the oven to 350 degrees F. Spray a 9-by-5-by-3-inch loaf pan with the cooking spray.

In a small bowl, combine the flour, baking powder, baking soda, and salt. Set this aside.

In a medium bowl, mix together the sugar, margarine or butter, and eggs. Coat the bananas with the lemon juice prior to mashing to keep them from turning brown as they bake. Stir the buttermilk and mashed bananas into the sugar mixture. Add the flour mixture to the banana mixture and stir until the flour is just moistened. Do not overmix. Add the nuts, if desired. Pour the batter into the prepared loaf pan. Let it stand for 15 minutes before baking. Bake it for 50 to 60 minutes or until a toothpick inserted into the middle of the loaf comes out clean. The top will be golden brown.

Makes 12 servings (1 loaf).

Calories per serving: 195
Protein: 3 g
Carbohydrates: 32 g
Fat: 6 g
Cholesterol: 41 mg
Fiber: 1 g
Calcium: 37 mg

To balance your meal, add: fresh berries, low-fat milk

Creamy Chicken Salad

Roll up this salad in a tortilla or flat bread or stuff it into a tomato.

2 chicken breasts (about 6 ounces), boneless and skinless, grilled and sliced, or use 2 cups precooked chicken breast slices
⅓ cup light mayonnaise
2 green onions, thinly sliced
10 red or green seedless grapes, thinly sliced
½ teaspoon salt
dash black pepper

In a large bowl, toss all of the ingredients. Serve immediately or refrigerate until ready to serve.

Makes 4 servings.

Calories per serving: 150
Protein: 13 g
Carbohydrates: 5 g
Fat: 8 g
Cholesterol: 43 mg
Fiber: 0
Calcium: 10 mg

To balance your meal, add: celery and carrot sticks, fresh fruit cup

Tortilla Pinwheels

These are excellent for snacks or as an item for a lunch box. They keep well in the refrigerator for several days if tightly wrapped.

> 2 (8-inch) flour tortillas
> 1 tablespoon light cream cheese, softened
> 1 tablespoon honey mustard
> 2 very thin slices (shaved) ham or turkey
> 2 thin slices Swiss cheese

Spread the softened cream cheese lightly onto each tortilla. Then spread the honey mustard over the cream cheese. Place 1 ham or turkey slice onto each tortilla and top it with 1 slice of Swiss cheese.

Carefully roll up the tortillas in jelly-roll fashion. Wrap each roll in waxed paper, and close each end by twisting the paper. Chill the rolls in the refrigerator for at least two hours.

When the rolls are set, remove the wax paper and slice the rolls into 1-inch pinwheels or as desired.

Makes 2 servings.

3-WAY TORTILLA PINWHEEL VARIATIONS

#1: ½ cup cream cheese mixed with ¼ cup salsa.

#2: ½ cup cream cheese mixed with 2 tablespoons chopped green stuffed olives

#3: ½ cup pimento cheese

Spread the mixture onto each tortilla and follow the previous directions.

Calories per serving: 253
Protein: 12 g
Carbohydrates: 29 g
Fat: 10 g
Cholesterol: 24 mg
Fiber: 0
Calcium: 230 mg

To balance your meal, add:
Hearty Sweet and Sour Slaw*,
melon balls, or fruit of choice

Turkey Cheese Wrap

*You can't get much easier than this for a quick and tasty
lunch. Make a few wraps when you have extra time.
The entire family will love them.*

2 teaspoons herb-flavored cream cheese, softened
1 (8-inch) flour tortilla
1 ounce deli turkey, thinly sliced
1 ounce low-fat cheddar cheese, thinly sliced
¼ cup lettuce, shredded

Spread the cream cheese over the tortilla. Top it with turkey,
cheese, and lettuce. Roll it up tightly. Eat it immediately or wrap
it in plastic wrap, refrigerate, and store it for up to one day.

Makes 1 serving.

Calories per serving: 208
Protein: 17 g
Carbohydrates: 18 g
Fat: 8 g
Cholesterol: 25 mg
Fiber: 2 g
Calcium: 134 mg

*To balance your meal, add: baby carrots with
ranch dip, banana*

Avocado Chicken Salad Sandwiches

Here's a wonderful recipe for leftover chicken.

1 cup chicken, about 3 ounces, cooked and diced
½ cup celery, diced
¼ cup light mayonnaise
2 tablespoons avocado, diced
2 teaspoons lemon juice
dash each salt and black pepper
8 slices whole-grain bread or other bread of choice

In a medium bowl, combine all of the ingredients except the bread. Spread the mixture onto 4 slices of bread. Top it with remaining slices. Cut the sandwiches in half to serve.

Makes 4 servings.

Calories per serving: 215
Protein: 11 g
Carbohydrates: 30 g
Fat: 7 g
Cholesterol: 23 mg
Fiber: 10 g
Calcium: 211 mg

*To balance your meal, add: fruit salad,
Carrot Oatmeal Raisin Cookies**

Roast Beef and Cheese
Deli Wraps

A simple but favorite lunch that family members can make themselves. Kids enjoy these wraps as much as adults do.

> 2 (8-inch) flour tortillas
> 1 tablespoon light ranch dressing
> 2 thin slices deli roast beef
> 2 thin slices deli cheese, any variety
> 1 tomato, thinly sliced
> 2 large lettuce leaves

Warm the tortillas. Top them with ranch dressing, then layer the roast beef, cheese, tomato, and lettuce. Roll them up and secure them with toothpicks.

Makes 2 servings.

Calories per serving: 248
Protein: 23 g
Carbohydrates: 31 g
Fat: 8 g
Cholesterol: 19 mg
Fiber: 1 g
Calcium: 234 mg

To balance your meal, add: Creamy Tomato Soup,
Fruit Sorbet**

Crunchy Tuna Pita Pockets

This sandwich can be served warm or cold. If you desire, you can even add some shredded cheese on top.

    1 large pita, cut in half
    1 (6-ounce) can tuna, packed in water
    1 tablespoon light mayonnaise
    1 teaspoon Dijon mustard
    2 tablespoons water chestnuts, chopped

Cut and open the pita pockets. In a medium bowl, combine the tuna, mayonnaise, mustard, and water chestnuts. Fill each pocket equally.

Makes 2 servings.

Calories per serving: 224
Protein: 26 g
Carbohydrates: 19 g
Fat: 3 g
Cholesterol: 56 mg
Fiber: 1 g
Calcium: 30 mg

To balance your meal, add: Mom's Potato Soup,
fruit of choice*

Caesar Salad Pita

Here's a new way to enjoy the classic Caesar salad. Kids love it this way, too. If you are planning to take this for lunch, keep the dressing separate and add it just before you eat it.

    4 romaine lettuce leaves, torn
    2 teaspoons Parmesan cheese, grated
    ¼ cup croutons
    1 pita, cut in half
    2 tablespoons bottled Caesar salad dressing

Combine all ingredients, except the pita bread and dressing, in a large bowl. Toss. Divide and stuff into the pita halves. Pour the dressing over the top just before eating it.

Makes 2 servings.

Calories per serving: 163
Protein: 6 g
Carbohydrates: 20 g
Fat: 6 g
Cholesterol: 13 mg
Fiber: 1 g
Calcium: 86 mg

To balance your meal, add: fresh red and green pepper slices,
Margaret's Banana Bread*

BLT Tortillas

Try this easy modification to an old family favorite.

2 teaspoons light mayonnaise
2 slices bacon, crisp
2 lettuce leaves
½ tomato, thinly sliced
2 (8-inch) flour tortillas

Layer the mayonnaise, bacon, lettuce, and tomato onto each tortilla. Roll them up and secure them with toothpicks.

Makes 2 servings.

Calories per serving: 204
Protein: 7 g
Carbohydrates: 28 g
Fat: 7 g
Cholesterol: 8 mg
Fiber: 1 g
Calcium: 103 mg

To balance your meal, add: 5-Way Cream Soup (Broccoli)*,
Apple Streusel Bites*

Meatloaf Sandwiches

Use leftovers from Our Favorite Meat Loaf.
Add tomato, lettuce, and pickle slices, too, if
desired. Or top the sandwich with our Healthy
Sweet and Sour Cole Slaw in lieu of pickle slices.

    2 teaspoons light mayonnaise
    2 sourdough bread rolls
    2 thin slices leftover cooked beef or turkey meatloaf
    2 thin slices Swiss cheese
    4 dill pickle slices, if desired

Spread the mayonnaise over the bread rolls. Top them with the meatloaf, cheese, and pickle slices. Eat them immediately or wrap and take a sandwich to go.

Makes 2 servings.

Calories per serving: 268
Protein: 16 g
Carbohydrates: 27 g
Fat: 10 g
Cholesterol: 51 mg
Fiber: 1 g
Calcium: 155 mg

To balance your meal, add: Healthy Sweet and
Sour Cole Slaw*, fresh strawberries

Mini Pizza Bagels

These easy pizzas can be made in just a few minutes.
You can eat them right away or even freeze them to heat
them up in the toaster oven or the microwave later. For
quick cleanup, line the cookie sheet with foil.

> 4 mini bagels
> ½ cup marinara or pasta sauce
> 4 ounces part-skim mozzarella cheese, shredded

Preheat the oven or the toaster oven to 400 degrees F. Cut the
bagels in half. Spread each half with about 1 tablespoon of the
sauce. Sprinkle this with the shredded cheese. Place the bagels on
a cookie sheet. Bake them for 5 to 7 minutes until the bagels are
heated and the cheese is melted.

Makes 4 servings.

Calories per serving (2 bagel halves): 162
Protein: 10 g
Carbohydrates: 18 g
Fat: 5 g
Cholesterol: 16 mg
Fiber: 1 g
Calcium: 195 mg

To balance your meal, add: Freezer Cole Slaw*,
Popcorn Peanut Butter Delights*

Grilled Cheese Sandwich

There's nothing better than a grilled cheese sandwich.
Prepare a few that can easily be wrapped and
taken on the go. Also, check out our 5-Way
Grilled Cheese Sandwiches for fun variations.

1 teaspoon margarine
2 slices sourdough bread
2 slices light American cheese or other cheese of choice

Heat the margarine in a skillet over medium heat. Add the bread, topped with cheese, then top with remaining slice of bread. Cook it until the bread is light brown, then flip it to cook the other side. Eat the sandwich immediately or wrap it in foil to reheat later or eat cold.

Makes 1 sandwich.

Calories per serving: 242
Protein: 11 g
Carbohydrates: 27 g
Fat: 9 g
Cholesterol: 24 mg
Fiber: 1 g
Calcium: 241 mg

To balance your meal, add:
5-Way Cream Soup (Corn)*,
fruit of choice

5-WAY GRILLED CHEESE SANDWICH VARIATIONS

Follow the basic recipe, then try the following variations to please your family even more.

#1: Grilled Cheese and Tomato: Top the cheese with sliced tomatoes before topping with remaining bread slice.

#2: Turkey Grilled Cheese: Add turkey slices with cheese before topping with remaining bread slice.

#3: Ham Grilled Cheese: Add ham slices with cheese before topping with remaining bread slice.

#4: Mozzarella and Cheddar Grilled Cheese: Substitute mozzarella and cheddar cheeses for American.

#5: Tuna and Grilled Cheese: Add chunk tuna to the bread while it's cooking and top with cheese, and you'll have a tuna melt.

> ┌─────────────────────────┐
> │   **MEALS IN TEN**   │
> │   **MINUTES OR LESS**   │
> └─────────────────────────┘

Easy Burritos

Add your topping of choice, such as shredded lettuce,
chopped tomatoes, your favorite salsa, or all of these.
This can be a complete meal in itself.

> 1 can (10¾ ounces) chili or condensed chili beef soup
> 4 (10-inch) flour tortillas
> 1 cup taco, Mexican blend, or cheddar cheese, shredded

Spoon ¼ cup of the chili or the soup down the center of each tortilla. Top it with ¼ cup of the shredded cheese. Fold the sides over the filling, then fold the ends to close them. Place the burritos seam-side down on a microwavable plate. Microwave them for 2 minutes on high or until they're hot.

Makes 4 servings.

Calories per serving: 369
Protein: 15 g
Carbohydrates: 53 g
Fat: 8 g
Cholesterol: 12 mg
Fiber: 8 g
Calcium: 203 mg

To balance your meal, add: lettuce and tomato salad,
sliced mango

Cheesy Corn Chowder

*A quick and hearty soup to satisfy the youngest
to the oldest member of your family.*

1 (10¾-ounce) can condensed cream of potato soup
1½ cups low-fat (1%) milk
2 cups whole kernel corn
2 tablespoons sun-dried tomatoes, cut in strips
1 teaspoon dried onion flakes
½ cup cheddar cheese, shredded
black pepper (optional)

In a medium saucepan, mix together the soup, milk, corn, sun-dried tomatoes, and onion flakes. Heat this over medium heat to a boil. Cook on medium for 5 minutes. Stir in the cheese; simmer the chowder on low heat or until the cheese is melted. Season it with black pepper, if desired.

Makes 4 servings.

Calories per serving: 204
Protein: 10 g
Carbohydrates: 31 g
Fat: 4 g
Cholesterol: 12 mg
Fiber: 3 g
Calcium: 174 mg

*To balance your meal, add: whole wheat crackers,
fresh fruit of choice*

Tomato Tortellini Soup

Combine the children's favorites into one hearty soup
that is sure to be a hit in your home.

1 (10¾-ounce) can condensed tomato soup
1 soup can water
1 (8-ounce) package frozen tortellini
Parmesan cheese or other cheese of choice, grated,
    as desired

In a medium saucepan, combine the soup, water, and frozen tortellini. Heat this until the tortellini are tender. Sprinkle the soup with Parmesan cheese or another cheese of choice, as desired.

Makes 4 servings.

Calories per serving: 233
Protein: 10 g
Carbohydrates: 36 g
Fat: 5 g
Cholesterol: 21 mg
Fiber: 1 g
Calcium: 148 mg

To balance your meal, add: whole-grain breadsticks,
baby carrot sticks, low-fat milk

Quick Tomato Rice Soup

You can also use condensed gumbo soup in place of tomato soup, if you prefer.

1 (10¾-ounce) can condensed tomato soup
1 cup water
dash each garlic powder and onion powder
1¼ cups instant white rice

In a medium saucepan, combine the soup, water, garlic power, and onion powder over medium-high heat. Heat this to a boil. Stir in the rice and remove it from the heat. Let it stand 5 minutes. Fluff the rice with a fork before serving.

Makes 3 servings.

Calories per serving: 205
Protein: 4 g
Carbohydrates: 43 g
Fat: 2 g
Cholesterol: 0
Fiber: 1 g
Calcium: 22 mg

*To balance your meal, add: Grilled
Cheese Sandwich*, fresh strawberries*

Hamburger with Zest

*Here's a great option for that indoor grill. Quick, easy,
and ready in no time at all.*

> 1 pound extra lean ground beef or ground turkey
> 4 teaspoons prepared horseradish
> 2 teaspoons Dijon mustard
> ¼ teaspoon black pepper
> ¼ teaspoon seasoned salt
> 4 hamburger buns

In a medium bowl, combine the first five ingredients. Mix them
well. Shape the mixture into patties. Pan-fry, broil, or grill the
burgers (indoors or outdoors) and serve them on the buns.

Makes 4 servings.

Calories per serving: 266
Protein: 26 g
Carbohydrates: 22 g
Fat: 8 g
Cholesterol: 62 mg
Fiber: 1 g
Calcium: 69 mg

To balance your meal, add: Freezer Cole Slaw,
baked potato chips*

Pita Pizza

*Pita breads are typically considered a sandwich option,
but they can also be used for a quick pizza meal.*

2 pitas
½ cup pizza sauce
½ cup ripe olives, sliced and pitted
¼ cup sweet red pepper, finely chopped
½ cup mozzarella cheese, shredded
½ teaspoon dried oregano (optional)
dash garlic powder (optional)

Preheat the broiler. Place the pitas on an ungreased baking sheet.
Spread them with the pizza sauce, then top them with the olives
and red pepper. Sprinkle the cheese all over them. Add the
oregano and garlic powder, if desired. Set the pizzas under the
broiler for 3 minutes until the cheese is melted. Cut each pita in
half.

Makes 2 pitas, 4 servings of a half pita each.

Calories per serving: 141
Protein: 7 g
Carbohydrates: 21 g
Fat: 3 g
Cholesterol: 8 mg
Fiber: 1 g
Calcium: 132 mg

*To balance your meal, add: fresh green and
red pepper slices, applesauce cup*

Tortellini and Broccoli

Broccoli is a great addition to this quick meal, but you could also use frozen peas or mixed vegetables.

1 (8-ounce) package frozen tortellini
2 cups broccoli cuts, frozen
1 tablespoon Parmesan cheese, grated

In a medium saucepan, cook the frozen tortellini according to the package directions. Drain them.

Put the broccoli into a saucepan and steam or cook it according to the package directions. Drain it.

Combine the tortellini with the broccoli in large bowl. Top this with the grated Parmesan cheese. Serve immediately.

Makes 4 servings.

Calories per serving: 209
Protein: 11 g
Carbohydrates: 30 g
Fat: 5 g
Cholesterol: 22 mg
Fiber: 3 g
Calcium: 205 mg

To balance your meal, add: fruit cup, low-fat milk

Tuna Melt

*A favorite quick meal that can be made in the microwave
or the toaster oven in a flash.*

    2 English muffins, cut in half
    1 (6-ounce) can tuna packed in water, drained
    1 tablespoon light mayonnaise
    4 slices reduced-fat cheese of choice (cheddar,
        mozzarella, provolone, Swiss)

Lightly toast the English muffin halves. In a small bowl, combine
the tuna with the mayonnaise. Mix them well.

    Top the English muffin halves with the tuna. Lay a slice of
cheese over the top of each half. Put them in the microwave for 30
seconds or in a toaster oven for 2 minutes. Heat them until the
cheese is melted and the tuna is warm.

Makes 4 servings (half of an open-faced English muffin each).

Calories per serving: 170
Protein: 22 g
Carbohydrates: 8 g
Fat: 6 g
Cholesterol: 43 mg
Fiber: 0
Calcium: 379 mg

*To balance your meal, add: carrot and celery slices,
Orange Creamsicle Smoothie**

Taco Potatoes

*You don't need to make tacos to enjoy their great taste.
Try this variation for dinner tonight.*

2 medium potatoes
½ cup prepared salsa
2 tablespoons low-fat cheddar cheese, shredded
2 tablespoons light sour cream
4 tortilla chips, crushed

Put the potatoes in the microwave. Heat them on high for 5 to 6 minutes until they're cooked and soft. Slice the potatoes open across the tops. Lightly mash the potato with a fork. Spoon half of the salsa and cheese into each potato. Heat them in the microwave for 1 minute until the cheese is melted. Top them with the sour cream and crushed tortilla chips before serving.

Makes 2 servings.

Calories per serving: 199
Protein: 6 g
Carbohydrates: 37 g
Fat: 3 g
Cholesterol: 6 mg
Fiber: 3 g
Calcium: 76 mg

To balance your meal, add: fresh mango or pineapple slices

Chicken Caesar Wraps

*Wrap up the great taste of Caesar in your favorite
flatbread or tortilla.*

½ cup chicken (can use leftover chicken), cooked and
    chopped
1 cup romaine lettuce, chopped
1 tablespoon Parmesan cheese, grated
1 tablespoon prepared low-fat Caesar salad dressing
2 (8-inch) tortillas

In a small bowl, combine the chicken, lettuce, Parmesan cheese,
and salad dressing. Toss them well. Divide the mixture evenly and
place a portion in the center of each tortilla. Roll them up and eat
immediately.

Makes 2 servings.

Calories per serving: 243
Protein: 19 g
Carbohydrates: 27 g
Fat: 6 g
Cholesterol: 39 mg
Fiber: 0
Calcium: 159 mg

To balance your meal, add: watermelon balls, orange juice

Chicken Caesar Salad

Caesar salad is a favorite among children as well as adults. With the addition of chicken, it's hearty enough to be a meal by itself. You can even let the kids make it themselves.

> 4 chicken tenders, breaded, or 2 chicken fillets, lightly breaded
> 2 cups romaine lettuce, chopped
> 1 tablespoon Parmesan cheese, grated
> 2 tablespoons prepared low-fat Caesar salad dressing
> ½ cup croutons, any variety

Prepare the chicken according to the package directions. Cut it into strips. In a medium salad bowl, combine the lettuce, Parmesan cheese, salad dressing, and croutons. Toss these well. Top the salad with strips of chicken. Serve immediately.

Makes 2 servings.

Calories per serving: 149
Protein: 12 g
Carbohydrates: 20 g
Fat: 2 g
Cholesterol: 23 mg
Fiber: 3 g
Calcium: 72 mg

To balance your meal, add: italian breadsticks, fresh fruit

Vegetable Panini

Combine leftover veggies, or cut up a fresh assortment just to have on hand. What a great change of pace for dinner!

> 2 slices sourdough bread
> 1½ teaspoons prepared pesto sauce
> 1 slice low-fat mozzarella cheese
> 2 tablespoons red peppers, prepared, roasted
> 2 tomato slices
> cooking spray

Spread each slice of the bread with the prepared pesto. Layer the bottom slice with the cheese, red peppers, and tomato slices. Top this with the other slice of bread.

Spray a small skillet or an indoor grill with the cooking spray. Heat the skillet over medium heat, or heat the indoor grill following the manufacturer's directions. If you're preparing this in a skillet, cook the panini for 1 minute, then turn it over to cook the other side. If you're using an indoor grill, close it and heat the panini 1 to 2 minutes until the bread is lightly browned and the cheese is melted. Slice it in half to serve. Serve immediately.

Makes 1 serving.

Calories per serving: 227
Protein: 15 g
Carbohydrates: 30 grams
Fat: 5 g
Cholesterol: 7 mg
Fiber: 2 g
Calcium: 333 mg

*To balance your meal, add: prepared cole slaw,
dill pickles*

3-Way Vegetable Panini Variations

Follow the basic recipe, then try the following variations to suit your family's tastes.

#1: Provolone cheese, sun-dried tomatoes, artichoke hearts, red onion, and olive spread

#2: Sliced mushrooms, black and green ripe olives, and honey mustard spread

#3: Fresh basil leaves, green and red pepper slices, red onion, and Dijon mustard spread

Chicken Pesto Panini

*Keeping prepared pesto on hand will help you make a great
quick meal any time.*

> 2 slices Italian bread or focaccia
> 1½ teaspoons prepared pesto sauce
> 1 slice provolone cheese
> 2 tablespoons red peppers, prepared, roasted
> 1 chicken breast fillet, boneless, skinless, cooked* (about
> 3 ounces)
> cooking spray

Spread each slice of the bread with the prepared pesto. Layer the
bottom slice with the cheese, red peppers, and chicken. Top this
with the other slice of bread.

Spray a small skillet or an indoor grill with the cooking spray.
Heat the skillet over medium heat or heat the indoor grill following the manufacturer's directions. If you're preparing this in a skillet, cook the panini for 1 minute, then turn it over to cook the
other side. If you're using an indoor grill, close it and heat
the panini 1 to 2 minutes until the bread is lightly browned and the
cheese is melted. Slice it in half to serve. Serve immediately.

**If desired, you can cook your chicken breast fillet in the small skillet or on
the indoor grill prior to preparing your panini.*

Makes 1 serving.

Calories per serving: 367
Protein: 33 g
Carbohydrates: 32 g
Fat: 13 g
Cholesterol: 65 mg
Fiber: 2 g
Calcium: 466 mg

*To balance your meal, add: baked potato chips,
fresh pepper slices*

3-WAY MEAT PANINI VARIATIONS

Follow the basic recipe, then try the following variations to suit your family's tastes.

#1: Smoked turkey, smoked cheddar cheese, hot peppers, and prepared pesto

#2: Sliced salami, sliced pepperoni, red onion, mozzarella, and garlic-flavored olive oil

#3: Tuna fish, mozzarella cheese, artichoke hearts, and light mayonnaise or flavored mayonnaise

Turkey Artichoke Panini

Jazz up your leftover turkey or deli turkey with the great
tangy taste of artichoke.

> 2 slices Italian bread, sourdough, or focaccia
> 1 tablespoon prepared Dijon mustard
> 1 ounce deli turkey, sliced
> 2 artichoke hearts, sliced (canned or jarred)
> 1 slice low-fat provolone cheese
> cooking spray

Spread each slice of the bread with the prepared Dijon mustard. Layer the bottom slice with the turkey, artichoke hearts, and cheese. Top this with the other slice of bread.

Spray a small skillet or an indoor grill with the cooking spray. Heat the skillet over medium heat or heat the indoor grill following the manufacturer's directions. If you're preparing this in a skillet, cook the panini for 1 minute, then turn it over to cook the other side. If you're using an indoor grill, close it and heat the panini for 1 to 2 minutes until the bread is lightly browned and the cheese is melted. Slice it in half to serve. Serve immediately.

Makes 1 serving.

Calories per serving: 294
Protein: 21 g
Carbohydrates: 37 g
Fat: 9 g
Cholesterol: 27 mg
Fiber: 3 g
Calcium: 427 mg

To balance your meal, add: pretzel sticks, apple slices

Toasted Turkey Sub

You can be so much more creative with turkey and a hoagie bun than just making a cold sandwich. Try this variation.

1 hoagie bun or French roll
1½ teaspoons light mayonnaise
1 ounce deli turkey, sliced
lettuce leaves
2 slices tomatoes
2 slices red onion
2 slices green pepper
black olives, sliced, if desired
celery salt, if desired

Slice open the hoagie bun. Spread both sides of the bun with the mayonnaise. Layer it with the turkey, lettuce, tomatoes, red onion, green pepper, and olives, if desired. Sprinkle it with celery salt, if desired.

Wrap the sandwich in aluminum foil. Heat it in a toaster oven or a regular oven to your preferred degree of doneness.

Makes 1 serving.

Calories per serving: 270
Protein: 12 g
Carbohydrates: 38 g
Fat: 7 g
Cholesterol: 14 mg
Fiber: 3 g
Calcium: 93 mg

To balance your meal, add: cucumber slices, fresh grapes

Toasted Roast Beef and Cheese Sub

Toasted subs are all the rage now. You won't believe how easy they are to make at home.

1 hoagie bun or French roll
1½ teaspoons light mayonnaise
1 ounce deli roast beef, sliced
1 ounce deli low-fat Swiss cheese, or any other variety of choice, sliced
lettuce leaves
2 slices tomato

Slice open the hoagie bun. Spread both sides of the bun with the mayonnaise. Layer it with the roast beef, cheese, lettuce, and tomatoes.

Wrap the sandwich in aluminum foil. Heat it in a toaster oven or a regular oven to your preferred degree of doneness.

Makes 1 serving.

Calories per serving: 352
Protein: 21 g
Carbohydrates: 35 g
Fat: 14 g
Cholesterol: 36 mg
Fiber: 2 g
Calcium: 336 mg

To balance your meal, add: tortilla chips and salsa, fresh pear

30-MINUTE COUNT-DOWN TO DINNER

5-Way Chicken Breasts

Chicken breasts are the perfect quick food, especially when you start with boneless, skinless breasts. Here is a choice of five options for this favorite meal.

Honey Mustard Chicken

1 chicken breast (about 4 ounces), boneless, skinless
1 teaspoon honey
1 teaspoon Dijon mustard
dash each curry powder and soy sauce, if desired

Preheat the oven or the grill to 350 degrees F. Brush the chicken with the honey, mustard, curry powder, and soy sauce, if desired. Bake or grill it for 20 minutes until it's no longer pink inside.

Makes 1 serving.

Calories per serving: 149
Protein: 23 g
Carbohydrates: 6 g
Fat: 3 g
Cholesterol: 62 mg
Fiber: 0
Calcium: 18 mg

*To balance your meal, add: seasoned rice,
Oriental Spinach*, Fruit Sorbet**

Easy Baked Chicken

1 chicken breast (about 4 ounces), boneless, skinless
2 tablespoons low-calorie Italian salad dressing
2 tablespoons tomato juice
dash chili powder or hot pepper sauce

Preheat the oven or the grill to 350 degrees F. Brush the chicken with the salad dressing, tomato juice, and chili powder or hot pepper sauce, if desired. Bake or grill it for 20 minutes until it's no longer pink inside.

Makes 1 serving.

Calories per serving: 159
Protein: 23 g
Carbohydrates: 3 g
Fat: 5 g
Cholesterol: 64 mg
Fiber: 0
Calcium: 14 mg

To balance your meal, add:
Broccoli Rice*,
Apple Cinnamon Crisp*

Italian Chicken

1 chicken breast (about 4 ounces), boneless, skinless
2 tablespoons Italian bread crumbs
1 teaspoon vegetable oil

Roll the chicken breast in the crumbs. Heat the oil in a skillet over medium heat, then add the chicken. Sauté until it's done.

Makes 1 serving.

Calories per serving: 216
Protein: 25 g
Carbohydrates: 10 g
Fat: 7 g
Cholesterol: 62 mg
Fiber: 1 g
Calcium: 26 mg

To balance your meal, add:
Oven-Baked Eggplant*,
mixed green salad

Chicken Tarragon

1 chicken breast (about 4 ounces), boneless, skinless
¼ cup white wine
1 teaspoon dried tarragon leaves

Preheat the oven or the grill to 350 degrees F. Brush the chicken with the wine and tarragon leaves. Bake or grill the chicken for 20 minutes until it's no longer pink inside.

Makes 1 serving.

Calories per serving: 169
Protein: 23 g
Carbohydrates: 1 g
Fat: 3 g
Cholesterol: 62 mg
Fiber: 1 g
Calcium: 36 mg

To balance your meal, add:
Baked Potatoes Florentine*,
mixed fruit cup

Chicken Fajitas

1 chicken breast (about 4 ounces), boneless, skinless
½ teaspoon soy sauce
1 teaspoon lime juice
1 clove garlic, minced
1 8-inch flour tortilla
Mexican toppings: salsa, onions, chopped tomatoes, sour
    cream, as desired

Preheat the oven or the grill to 350 degrees F. Brush the chicken with the soy sauce, lime juice, and garlic. Bake or grill it for 20 minutes until it's no longer pink inside. Slice it and roll it up in a tortilla with your favorite Mexican salsa or toppings, as desired.

Makes 1 serving.

Calories per serving: 288
Protein: 28 g
Carbohydrates: 29 g
Fat: 6 g
Cholesterol: 62 mg
Fiber: 2 g
Calcium: 37 mg

To balance your meal, add:
steamed rice,
fresh pineapple slices

Oven-Fried Chicken

Make this dish ahead of time with chicken pieces (legs, thighs, breasts), cool them in the refrigerator, and take them along to a ball game or for dinner on the run.

> 6 chicken breasts (about 4 ounces each), boneless, skinless
> ¼ cup flour
> cooking spray
> 2 eggs
> ½ teaspoon salt
> ½ teaspoon paprika
> ½ teaspoon garlic salt
> 1 tablespoon honey
> ¾ cup seasoned bread crumbs

Preheat the oven to 325 degrees F. Place the chicken breasts inside a resealable plastic bag. Add the flour and shake well.

Spray a 9-by-13-inch baking pan with the cooking spray. In a small bowl, mix together the eggs, salt, paprika, garlic salt, and honey. Put the bread crumbs in a shallow bowl or a pie pan.

Dip the floured chicken into the egg mixture, then into the bread crumbs. Place the chicken on a baking sheet.

Bake it for 25 minutes or until the chicken is tender and no longer pink inside.

Makes 6 servings.

Calories per serving: 229
Protein: 27 g
Carbohydrates: 18 g
Fat: 4 g
Cholesterol: 125 mg
Fiber: 1 g
Calcium: 35 mg

To balance your meal, add: Mashed Potatoes (or Not),
Dilled Green Beans**

My Own Chicken Soup

Homemade chicken soup is easier than ever. Keep the ingredients on hand for an easy-to-make comfort food.

1 tablespoon vegetable oil
½ pound fresh mushrooms, sliced
1 onion, chopped
1 carrot, thinly sliced
1 stalk celery, thinly sliced
4 cans (14½ ounces each) chicken broth
1 pound chicken breasts, boneless, skinless, diced
1 garlic clove, minced
¼ pound seashell pasta
2 plum tomatoes, diced
1 tablespoon dried parsley flakes

Heat the oil in a Dutch oven over medium heat. Add the mushrooms, onions, carrot, and celery. Cook until the vegetables are tender.

Add the broth, chicken, and garlic to the pot. Bring this to a boil, then reduce the heat to a simmer. Cover the pot and cook the soup for 15 minutes. Add the pasta, tomatoes, and parsley. Cook the soup 5 to 8 minutes more.

Makes 10 cups.

Calories per serving: 192
Protein: 15 g
Carbohydrates: 23 g
Fat: 4 g
Cholesterol: 25 mg
Fiber: 2 g
Calcium: 19 mg

To balance your meal, add: Italian Bread Knots*,
fresh fruit cup

Chicken Quesadillas

For a variation, try this recipe using sliced beef.

2 chicken breasts (about 8 ounces), skinless, boneless,
    diced
½ teaspoon chili powder
¼ teaspoon salt
¼ teaspoon black pepper
2 tablespoons vegetable oil, divided
½ pound mushrooms, sliced
3 plum tomatoes, diced
6 (8-inch) flour tortillas
¾ cup cheese, any variety, shredded
prepared salsa (optional)

Sprinkle the chicken with the chili powder, salt, and black pepper.

Heat half of the oil in a large skillet. Add the chicken. Cook it 3 to 4 minutes or until it's no longer pink. Remove it from the skillet.

Heat the remaining oil in the skillet. Add the mushrooms and diced tomatoes. Cook these, stirring frequently, for about 3 minutes. Remove them from the skillet. Wipe out the skillet.

Heat the dry skillet over medium heat. Place 1 tortilla in the skillet. Add 2 tablespoons of the shredded cheese, one-third of the chopped chicken, one-third of the mushroom-tomato mixture, and another 2 tablespoons of the shredded cheese. Cook this until the cheese melts. Top it with the second tortilla. Flip the tortillas and cook them until both sides begin to get crispy. Remove the quesadilla from skillet.

Continue with the remaining tortillas and ingredients. Cut each quesadilla into 6 wedges. Serve them with salsa, if desired.

Makes 18 wedges, about 3 to 4 servings.

Calories per wedge: 80
Protein: 5 g
Carbohydrates: 6 g
Fat: 4 g
Cholesterol: 8 mg
Fiber: 1 g
Calcium: 36 mg

To balance your meal, add: Creamy Tomato Soup*,
Apple Cinnamon Crisp*

Italian Chicken Rolls

Serve these rolls with a marinara dipping sauce if you choose.

> 4 chicken breasts (about 4 ounces each), skinless,
>   boneless
> cooking spray
> 1 tomato, finely chopped
> 2 tablespoons Parmesan cheese, grated
> ¼ teaspoon oregano
> dash black pepper
> 1 egg white, beaten
> 1 tablespoon water
> ½ cup seasoned bread crumbs

Pound the chicken breasts to ¼-inch thick. Spray a 2-quart baking dish with the cooking spray. Preheat the oven to 400 degrees F.

In a small bowl, combine the chopped tomato, Parmesan cheese, oregano, and pepper. Spread the mixture over the flattened chicken breasts. Roll up the chicken and secure it with a toothpick.

In a pie pan or a flat bowl, beat the egg white with the water. Put the bread crumbs in another pie pan. Dip the chicken rolls in the egg mixture, then roll them in the bread crumbs to coat them.

Place the chicken seam-side down in the prepared baking dish. Bake it for 20 to 25 minutes or until the chicken is tender and no longer pink inside. Remove the toothpicks to serve it.

Makes 4 servings.

Calories per roll: 199
Protein: 27 g
Carbohydrates: 11 g
Fat: 4 g
Cholesterol: 65 mg
Fiber: 1 g
Calcium: 72 mg

To balance your meal, add: Broccoli Rice,
mandarin orange slices*

Sweet and Sour Glazed Chicken

This recipe works great on the grill, too,
both indoors and outdoors.

4 chicken breasts (about 4 ounces each), boneless,
  skinless
salt and black pepper, as desired
1 teaspoon garlic, minced
1 teaspoon lime juice
1 teaspoon lemon juice
2 tablespoons balsamic vinegar
2 tablespoons Dijon mustard
¼ cup light brown sugar
⅓ cup honey

Preheat the oven to 350 degrees F.

Sprinkle the chicken breasts with the salt and black pepper as desired. Place the chicken in a baking dish.

In a small bowl, combine the remaining ingredients. Mix them well. Brush the chicken generously with the sauce. Bake it for 20 to 30 minutes until the chicken is no longer pink inside.

Makes 4 servings.

Calories per serving: 274
Protein: 23 g
Carbohydrates: 39 g
Fat: 3 g
Cholesterol: 62 mg
Fiber: 0
Calcium: 39 mg

To balance your meal, add: wild rice, green beans,
fresh pineapple slices

Chicken Artichoke Casserole

Jazz up your chicken dinner with the great taste of artichokes.
Your family will thank you for it.

cooking spray
1 tablespoon margarine or butter
¼ cup chopped green onions
1 clove garlic, minced
4 chicken breasts (about 4 ounces each), boneless,
    skinless, cut into strips
3 tablespoons flour
2 cups low-fat milk
¾ cup cheddar cheese, shredded
1 cup mushrooms, sliced
1 (12-ounce) jar artichoke hearts, drained and halved

Preheat the oven to 350 degrees F. Spray a baking dish with the cooking spray.

In a large skillet, heat the margarine or butter over medium heat. Add the onions and garlic. Add the chicken. Cook it for 3 to 4 minutes until the chicken is no longer pink. Remove the chicken. Stir in the flour. Heat it until it's bubbly. Reduce the heat to low. Slowly add the milk and cook it until the mixture thickens, stirring constantly. Return the chicken to the skillet. Add the cheese, mushrooms, and artichokes.

Pour the mixture into the prepared baking dish. Bake it for 20 to 30 minutes.

Makes 6 servings.
Calories per serving: 268
Protein: 24 g
Carbohydrates: 14 g
Fat: 13 g
Cholesterol: 65 mg
Fiber: 2 g
Calcium: 202 mg

To balance your meal, add:
Fruity Acorn Squash*,
Summer Dessert*

Crunchy Chicken

Use prepackaged chicken strips to save additional time.

cooking spray
1 (7-ounce) bag baked potato chips
½ teaspoon cayenne pepper
¼ teaspoon salt
2 eggs
2 pounds (about 8) chicken breasts, boneless, skinless, cut
    into 1½-inch pieces
chili sauce, ranch dressing, honey mustard, if desired, for
    dipping

Preheat the oven to 450 degrees F. Spray a baking sheet with the
cooking spray.

Crush half of the potato chips into fine crumbs, the other half
into coarser crumbs. Mix in the cayenne pepper and salt. In a separate bowl, whisk the eggs.

Dip the chicken pieces into the eggs, then firmly press them
into the potato chips. Place the chicken in a single layer on a baking sheet. Bake it for 10 minutes.

Put the dipping sauce of choice in a small bowl. Serve it with
the browned chicken pieces.

Makes 8 servings.

Calories per serving (without dipping sauce): 273
Protein: 26 g
Carbohydrates: 13 g
Fat: 12 g
Cholesterol: 116 mg
Fiber: 1 g
Calcium: 23 mg

To balance your meal, add: Carrot Fries*, Freezer Slaw*

Chicken Nachos

*Serve these as an occasional treat for a quick lunch or
dinner or, better yet, as an appetizer or a snack. Try
them made with lean ground beef, too.*

1 (8–10-ounce) bag tortilla chips
1 cup chicken (about 2 breasts, 3–4 ounces each), diced,
    cooked
¾ cup low-fat cheddar or taco-flavored cheese, shredded
½ cup prepared salsa
¼ cup ripe olives

Arrange the tortilla chips on a microwavable platter. Top them
with the chicken, cheese, salsa, and olives. Cook the nachos in a
microwave on high for 3 minutes, until the cheese is melted.

Makes 6 servings.

Calories per serving: 234
Protein: 13 g
Carbohydrates: 29 g
Fat: 8 g
Cholesterol: 20 mg
Fiber: 2 g
Calcium: 132 mg

To balance your meal, add: Hearty Sweet and Sour Slaw*

Chicken and Capers

Such a simple and tasty dish! Capers will keep for a long time in the refrigerator and are very good for jazzing up meals.

cooking spray
½ cup flour
2 teaspoons paprika
½ teaspoon black pepper
¼ teaspoon salt
1 teaspoon garlic powder
4 chicken breasts (about 4 ounces each), boneless, skinless
½ cup dry white wine
½ cup chicken broth
2 teaspoons capers, drained
2 teaspoons fresh parsley, chopped

Preheat the oven to 450 degrees F. Spray a baking dish with the cooking spray.

In a small pie pan, combine the flour with the seasonings. Dredge the chicken in the flour mixture. Place the chicken in the prepared baking dish. Pour the wine and broth over the chicken. Sprinkle it with the capers. Cover it with foil and bake it for 15 minutes. Reduce the heat to 325 degrees F and continue baking until the chicken is tender, about 10 to 15 minutes longer. Sprinkle it with the chopped parsley and serve.

Makes 4 servings.

Calories per serving: 209
Protein: 25 g
Carbohydrates: 14 g
Fat: 3 g
Cholesterol: 62 mg
Fiber: 1 g
Calcium: 21 mg

To balance your meal, add:
hot cooked spaghetti,
steamed broccoli florets

Sesame Noodles in Peanut Sauce

These are a hit with kids and adults alike.

1 pound thin spaghetti, uncooked
½ cup smooth peanut butter
1–2 garlic cloves
⅓ cup soy sauce
⅓ cup rice vinegar
1 teaspoon sesame oil
1 cucumber, julienned
2 carrots, peeled and shredded

Cook the spaghetti according to the package directions. Drain it and transfer it into a large bowl. Set it aside.

In a blender container, combine the peanut butter, garlic, soy sauce, vinegar, and sesame oil. Blend until this is smooth.

Toss the peanut sauce with the spaghetti. Add the cucumber and carrots.

Makes 8 servings.

Calories per serving: 328
Protein: 12 g
Carbohydrates: 49 g
Fat: 10 g
Cholesterol: 0
Fiber: 3 g
Calcium: 27 mg

To balance your meal, add: mixed green salad,
Cheese Biscuits*

Quick and Easy Vegetable Stir-Fry

*Stir-frying is a quick, easy, and healthful way
to cook vegetables, meats, and more. You can use
a wok or a skillet, whatever you prefer. Keep
precut vegetables on hand for busy days.*

1 tablespoon vegetable oil
1 clove garlic, minced
¼ teaspoon powdered ginger or 1 tablespoon fresh ginger,
    grated
2 cups vegetables (broccoli, cauliflower, onions, peppers,
    squash), raw, sliced
1 teaspoon soy sauce

In a large skillet over medium-high heat, heat the oil. Add the garlic and ginger. Stir-fry these for 15 seconds. Add the vegetables and soy sauce. Stir-fry them an additional 3 to 5 minutes, stirring constantly.

If you choose to include chicken or beef in the dish, add an additional tablespoon of oil to the recipe ingredients. First, stir-fry the meat until it's browned and cooked throughout. Remove the meat to a plate. Next, stir-fry the vegetables. When they are tender, add the meat back to the skillet.

Makes 2 servings.

Calories per serving: 120
Protein: 3 g
Carbohydrates: 13 g
Fat: 7 g
Cholesterol: 0
Fiber: 4 g
Calcium: 44 mg

To balance your meal, add: Crunchy Tuna Pita Pocket,
apple wedges*

Eggplant Bake

Using low-fat cottage cheese in place of ricotta cheese
can reduce the amount of fat in this recipe with
little change of taste.

2 eggplants, sliced
1 tablespoon vegetable oil
salt and black pepper to taste
1 (16-ounce) container low-fat cottage cheese or ricotta
   cheese
2 eggs
½ cup Parmesan cheese, grated
½ cup part-skim mozzarella cheese, shredded
2 teaspoons oregano
1 (16-ounce) jar pasta sauce

Preheat the oven to 425 degrees F.

Arrange the eggplant slices on a cookie sheet. Brush them with the oil and season them with the salt and black pepper, as desired. Roast them about 8 to 10 minutes until they're tender, turning them once. Remove them from the oven and transfer them onto a plate. Reduce the heat to 375 degrees F.

In a large bowl, combine the ricotta cheese, eggs, ¼ cup of the Parmesan and mozzarella cheeses, oregano, and additional salt and black pepper, if desired.

Spread about ½ cup of the pasta sauce on the bottom of a 9-by-13-inch baking dish. Top this with a single layer of the roasted eggplant. Layer it with the cheese mixture. Continue layering until all the ingredients are used up, ending with the cheese mixture. Sprinkle this with the remaining Parmesan and mozzarella cheese. Bake it for about 18 to 20 minutes, until it's golden brown and bubbly.

Makes 8 servings.

Calories per serving: 188
Protein: 14 g
Carbohydrates: 16 g
Fat: 8 g
Cholesterol: 63 mg
Fiber: 4 g
Calcium: 210 mg

To balance your meal, add: 5-Way Chicken Breast (Italian)*,
melon cup

Pull-Apart Pizza

*Add toppings of your choice, such as diced green pepper,
sliced mushrooms or olives, chopped pepperoni,
broccoli florets, or spinach.*

cooking spray
1 (11½-ounce) package refrigerated bread rolls
½ cup pasta sauce
1 cup part-skim mozzarella cheese, shredded

Preheat the oven to 375 degrees F. Spray a 9-inch pie pan with the cooking spray.

Remove the rolls from the package. Cut each roll in half. Pack the rolls tightly into the prepared pie pan. Drizzle the sauce over the bread dough. Sprinkle it with the toppings and shredded cheese.

Bake the pizza for 10 minutes until the dough turns golden brown and the cheese is melted.

Makes 6 servings.

Calories per serving: 209
Protein: 10 g
Carbohydrates: 27 g
Fat: 6 g
Cholesterol: 11 mg
Fiber: 1 g
Calcium: 126 mg

To balance your meal, add: Southwestern Corn Salad,
watermelon wedge*

French Bread Pizza

*If you are in a hurry and don't have a frozen pizza on hand,
there's always French Bread Pizza. Add your choice of
toppings and enjoy. You could also make it with
ground beef left over from another night.*

1 small loaf French bread (5-by-2-inch), halved
1 teaspoon olive oil
¼ cup spaghetti or pasta sauce
1 tablespoon Parmesan cheese, grated
¼ cup fresh mushrooms, sliced
¼ cup green pepper, chopped
2 tablespoons onions, chopped
¼ cup part skim shredded mozzarella cheese, shredded

Preheat the oven to 350 degrees F. Slice the bread in half lengthwise. Brush the oil over the bread. Place the bread under the broiler for 1 minute or until it's browned.

Spread the sauce on the bread and top it with the remaining ingredients. Bake the pizza for 10 minutes or until the cheese is melted.

Makes 2 servings.

Calories per serving: 337
Protein: 14 g
Carbohydrates: 50 g
Fat: 9 g
Cholesterol: 10 mg
Fiber: 4 g
Calcium: 222 mg

To balance your meal, add: mixed green salad, Fruit Sorbet*

Family Favorite Pasta Bar

The possibilities are endless.

Start with	Toss with	Add	Top with
penne pasta	marinara sauce	broccoli	Romano cheese
spaghetti	Alfredo sauce	spinach	shredded mozzarella
ravioli	vodka sauce	mushrooms	grated Parmesan cheese
tortellini	olive oil	artichoke hearts	feta cheese
angel hair pasta	tomato basil sauce	onions	chopped fresh parsley
rotini	garden vegetable sauce	olives	cherry tomatoes
pasta shells	meat sauce	roasted red peppers	shredded Colby cheese
mostaccioli	pesto sauce	pine nuts	grated Romano-Parmesan combo

Easy Classic Chili
with Spaghetti

You can add other toppings such as sour cream, green onions,
or tortilla chips to suit everyone's taste in your family.

>   10 ounces spaghetti or macaroni noodles, uncooked
>   1 teaspoon oil
>   1 pound lean ground beef
>   1 medium onion, chopped
>   1 clove garlic, minced
>   1 (26-ounce) jar pasta sauce, any variety
>   1 (15-ounce) can kidney beans, rinsed and drained
>   2 tablespoons chili powder
>   ½ cup low-fat cheddar cheese, shredded (optional)

Prepare the pasta according to the package directions. Drain it.
    Heat the oil in a large skillet. Cook the ground beef, onion, and
garlic until the beef is browned. Drain the excess fat from the skillet. Add the pasta sauce, beans, and chili powder. Reduce the heat
to low and cook the sauce an additional 5 to 8 minutes until it's
cooked throughout.
    Serve the sauce over the spaghetti. Sprinkle it with the shred-
ded cheese, if desired.

Makes 8 servings.

Calories per serving: 342
Protein: 21 g
Carbohydrates: 45 g
Fat: 8 g
Cholesterol: 21 mg
Fiber: 6 g
Calcium: 65 mg

To balance your meal, add: tossed green salad,
fruit cocktail cup

Angel Hair Pasta Supreme

*Add steamed clams, jumbo shrimp, scallops, or slices of
cooked chicken breast. If fresh basil is not available,
look for refrigerated herb tubes in the produce section.*

1 (8-ounce) package angel hair pasta
1 tablespoon olive oil
2 cloves garlic, minced
¼ cup green onions, sliced
3 large tomatoes, peeled and diced
2 tablespoons fresh basil, chopped
1 teaspoon salt
¼ teaspoon black pepper, coarsely ground
¼ cup Parmesan cheese, freshly grated

Cook the pasta according to the package directions. Drain it.
    In a large skillet, heat the olive oil. Add the garlic and onions.
Cook them until they're tender, but not brown. Add the tomatoes,
basil, salt, and pepper; cook, stirring constantly, for 2 minutes.
    Put the warm pasta on a platter and pour the tomato mixture
over the pasta. Sprinkle it with the cheese.

Makes 4 servings.

Calories per serving: 254
Protein: 11 g
Carbohydrates: 39 g
Fat: 7 g
Cholesterol: 5 mg
Fiber: 3 g
Calcium: 102 mg

To balance your meal, add: Nutty Broccoli,
fresh pineapple slices*

Sloppy Pizza Burgers

*Try this new version of the old standby pizza dinner.
Your family will love it.*

1 pound lean ground beef
1 small onion, chopped
1 (14-ounce) jar pasta sauce
8 hamburger buns
¾ cup part-skim mozzarella cheese, shredded

In a large skillet, brown the ground beef with the onion. Drain the excess fat. Add the pasta sauce and cook the meat and onions throughout.

Spoon the hamburger mixture onto the buns. Top them with shredded cheese. Serve them immediately.

Makes 8 servings.

Calories per serving: 248
Protein: 18 g
Carbohydrates: 22 g
Fat: 9 g
Cholesterol: 27 mg
Fiber: 2 g
Calcium: 131 mg

To balance your meal, add: Carrot Fries*, melon slices

Cheesy Mac and Cheese

Here's a favorite classic with kids and adults. This easy-to-prepare dish will sell you on homemade mac and cheese over any package mix. Check out our 5-Way Mac and Cheese variations that follow.

cooking spray
6 cups macaroni noodles (shells, ziti, elbow), cooked, hot
  (about 3 cups uncooked)
¼ cup flour
2 cups low-fat milk
1 cup low-fat cheddar cheese, shredded
6 ounces processed cheese food, cubed

Preheat the oven to 350 degrees F. Spray a 2-quart casserole dish with the cooking spray. Prepare the macaroni according to package directions. Set aside.

Heat a large saucepan over medium heat, add the flour, and gradually add the milk, stirring with a whisk until it's well blended. Cook the mixture until it thickens, about 5 minutes. Add half of the cheddar cheese and all of the processed cheese. Cook everything for 3 minutes or until the cheeses are melted. Remove it from the heat. Stir in the cooked macaroni noodles.

Spoon the mixture into the prepared casserole dish. Top it with the remaining cheddar cheese. Bake it for 20 minutes or until it's bubbly.

Makes 8 servings.

Calories per serving (for Cheesy Mac and Cheese without variations): 295
Protein: 15 g
Carbohydrates: 38 g
Fat: 8 g
Cholesterol: 26 mg
Fiber: 1 g
Calcium: 252 mg

To balance your meal, add: Oven Baked Eggplant,
Summer Dessert**

5-WAY MAC AND CHEESE VARIATIONS

Follow the basic recipe, then try the following variations to suit your family's tastes.

#1: Broccoli Mac and Cheese: Add 1 cup of chopped broccoli to the boiling pasta during the last 2 minutes of cooking. Drain. Add to the cheese mixture as directed.

#2: Chicken Mac and Cheese: Add 1 cup of precooked chicken pieces to the hot cheese mixture.

#3: Beef and Salsa Mac and Cheese: Brown ½ pound of ground beef and drain the fat. Add it to the hot cheese mixture, along with ½ cup of prepared salsa.

#4: Tuna Mac and Cheese: Add 1 (6-ounce) can of chunk tuna, drained, or 1 pouch of tuna to the cheese mixture.

#5: Mixed Vegetable Mac and Cheese: Add 1 cup of thawed, frozen mixed vegetables to the cheese mixture.

Baked Potatoes Florentine

Tired of the same old baked potato? Try this one as a change of pace. You can also add shredded cheese on top, if desired.

2 large baking potatoes
1 cup spinach, chopped, frozen
2 teaspoons margarine or butter
1 slice bacon (optional)

Bake the potatoes in a microwave until they're tender, about 5 to 6 minutes. Cut them in half lengthwise after baking, scoop out the potato, and place the pulp in a mixing bowl.

Preheat the oven to 350 degrees F. Steam the spinach in a microwave according to the package directions and drain the excess liquid. Add the spinach and margarine or butter to the potato pulp and mix them until they're well-blended. Spoon the potato and spinach mixture into the potato skin shells.

If you're using bacon, cook the bacon until it's crisp. Crumble and sprinkle it over the stuffed potatoes.

Heat the potatoes in the oven for 15 to 20 minutes until they're cooked throughout.

Makes 2 servings.

Calories per serving: 185
Protein: 5 g
Carbohydrates: 34 g
Fat: 4 g
Cholesterol: 4 mg
Fiber: 5 g
Calcium: 100 mg

To balance your meal, add: Baked Fish Supreme*,
lemon sherbet

Fettuccine Broccoli Alfredo

*Add chopped cooked chicken to this dish for a complete meal.
Look for low-fat half-and-half to reduce the fat, if desired.*

12 ounces fettuccine noodles, uncooked
2 cups broccoli, frozen, chopped
2 tablespoons margarine or butter
¼ cup low-fat half-and-half
½ cup Parmesan cheese, grated

Prepare the fettuccine according to the package directions. Add
the broccoli to the pasta during the last 2 minutes of cooking.
Drain.

In a small saucepan over medium-low heat, combine the margarine or butter, half-and-half, and Parmesan cheese. Toss this
with the noodles and the cooked broccoli and serve it.

Makes 6 servings.

Calories per serving: 256
Protein: 11 g
Carbohydrates: 35 g
Fat: 8 g
Cholesterol: 15 mg
Fiber: 3 g
Calcium: 157 mg

*To balance your meal, add: baked chicken breasts,
Italian Bread Knots*, fresh fruit of choice*

Spaghetti with Clam Sauce

The wonderful flavors of clams, Parmesan cheese, and garlic make this a great pasta dish, and it's so easy.

1 (6½-ounce) can clams
water, as needed
2 teaspoons cornstarch
1 tablespoon olive oil
1 clove garlic, minced
2 tablespoons onion, chopped
¼ teaspoon basil
1 tablespoon fresh parsley, chopped
1 tablespoon Parmesan cheese, grated
2 cups spaghetti, cooked, hot

Drain and reserve the clam juice. Add the water to the clam juice to make 1 cup. Stir in the cornstarch. Set it aside.

In a large skillet, heat the oil over medium heat. Sauté the garlic, onion, basil, and parsley. Add the clam juice mixture and cook it until it's thickened, about 1 to 2 minutes. Stir in the Parmesan cheese and clams. Heat everything thoroughly. Pour this over the hot spaghetti.

Makes 2 servings.

Calories per serving: 282
Protein: 9 g
Carbohydrates: 44 g
Fat: 8 g
Cholesterol: 11 mg
Fiber: 2 g
Calcium: 80 mg

*To balance your meal, add: lettuce wedge with dressing,
Apple Cinnamon Crisp**

Chinese Pepper Steak

This old classic is a favorite in many homes.

1 tablespoon vegetable oil
½ teaspoon salt
black pepper to taste
1 pound sirloin steak, boneless, thinly sliced
¼ cup onions, chopped
1 clove garlic, minced
1 cup celery, diced
3 medium green peppers, sliced
1 cup beef broth
2 tablespoons cornstarch
¼ cup water
2 tablespoons soy sauce

In a large skillet, heat the oil over medium heat. Add the salt and black pepper. Add the sliced steak. Cook it until the beef is browned. Add the onions and garlic. Cook until they're tender. Stir in the celery and peppers. Cook everything for 2 minutes more. Add the broth. Cover the skillet and cook the meat and vegetables over medium-low heat until they are tender, about 20 minutes.

Blend the cornstarch with the water and soy sauce. Add this to the meat mixture. Stir it until the sauce is thickened.

Makes 6 servings.

Calories per serving: 212
Protein: 25 g
Carbohydrates: 8 g
Fat: 8 g
Cholesterol: 67 mg
Fiber: 2 g
Calcium: 25 mg

To balance your meal, add: white or brown rice,
tossed salad, mango slices

Steak and Pepper Fajita Wraps

Try this dish with thinly sliced chicken strips, too.

2 teaspoons vegetable oil
1 pound beef flank steak, cut into strips
2 large bell peppers, green, red, or yellow, thinly sliced
1 large onion, thinly sliced
8 (8-inch) flour tortillas
½ cup prepared salsa

Heat 1 teaspoon of the oil in a large skillet over medium heat. Add the beef. Stir-fry until it's cooked thoroughly. Remove the beef and set it aside. Add the remaining oil to the skillet. Stir-fry the vegetables until they're tender crisp. Remove the vegetables.

Warm the tortillas, if desired, in a microwave. To serve, place the beef strips, vegetables, and salsa in each tortilla and roll it up.

Makes 8 servings.

Calories per tortilla: 224
Protein: 17 g
Carbohydrates: 20 g
Fat: 9 g
Cholesterol: 29 mg
Fiber: 3 g
Calcium: 13 mg

*To balance your meal, add: mini egg rolls,
mandarin oranges*

5-Way Fish Fillet

Get hooked on fish by trying these foolproof ways to cook a fish fillet. Fish of your choice could include catfish, whitefish, mahi mahi, tilapia, and so on.

Crispy Oven-Fried Fish

cooking spray
½-inch-thick fish fillet (4 ounces raw)
1 teaspoon margarine, melted
1 tablespoon flour
¼ teaspoon paprika
salt and black pepper to taste

Preheat the oven to 350 degrees F. Spray a baking dish with the cooking spray.

Rub the fish with the margarine, then sprinkle it with the flour, paprika, salt, and black pepper. Place the fillet in the prepared baking dish. Bake it for 20 minutes until it flakes easily with a fork.

Makes 1 serving.

Calories per serving: 167
Protein: 22 g
Carbohydrates: 6 g
Fat : 5 g
Cholesterol: 58 mg
Fiber: 0
Calcium: 23 mg

To balance your meal, add: Broccoli Rice*, tossed salad

Fish with Tomato Cheese Topping

cooking spray
½-inch-thick fish fillet (4 ounces raw)
1 teaspoon margarine, melted
1 teaspoon lemon juice
1 tablespoon onion, chopped
½ cup fresh tomato, chopped
1 tablespoon Parmesan cheese, grated

Preheat the oven to 350 degrees F. Spray a baking dish with the cooking spray.

Place the fish in the baking dish. Top it with the remaining ingredients, except for the cheese. Bake it for 20 minutes or until the fish flakes easily with a fork. When it's done, sprinkle it with the cheese.

Makes 1 serving.

Calories per serving: 189
Protein: 25 g
Carbohydrates: 6 g
Fat: 7 g
Cholesterol: 63 mg
Fiber: 1 g
Calcium: 114 mg

To balance your meal, add:
wild rice pilaf,
cantaloupe wedge

Baked Fish with Herbs

cooking spray
½-inch-thick fish fillet (4 ounces raw)
1 teaspoon margarine, melted
1 teaspoon fresh parsley, chopped
1 teaspoon chives
¼ teaspoon tarragon
paprika, garlic powder, thyme, salt, and black pepper
     to taste

Preheat the oven to 350 degrees F. Spray a baking dish with the cooking spray.

Place the fish in the baking dish. Top it with the remaining ingredients. Bake it for 20 minutes or until the fish flakes easily with a fork.

Makes 1 serving.

Calories per serving: 142
Protein: 21 g
Carbohydrates: 0
Fat: 5 g
Cholesterol: 58 mg
Fiber: 0
Calcium: 38 mg

To balance your meal, add:
Sweet Potatoes and Apples*,
steamed green beans

Barbecued Fish in Foil

$\frac{1}{2}$-inch-thick fish fillet (4 ounces)
1 tablespoon barbecue sauce

Preheat the oven to 350 degrees F.

Place the fish on a greased sheet of aluminum foil. Cover it with the barbecue sauce. Bake it for 20 minutes or until the fish flakes easily with a fork.

Makes 1 serving.

Calories per serving: 114
Protein: 21 g
Carbohydrates: 2 g
Fat: 2 g
Cholesterol: 54 mg
Fiber: 0
Calcium: 23 mg

To balance your meal, add: corn on the cob, cole slaw

Grilled Salmon Fillet

1 salmon fillet (4 ounces raw)
1 teaspoon lemon juice
½ teaspoon soy sauce

Marinate the salmon in the lemon juice and soy sauce for 25 minutes. Grill or broil it for 5 to 10 minutes until cooked throughout.

Makes 1 serving.

Calories per serving: 137
Protein: 23 g
Carbohydrates: 1 g
Fat: 4 g
Cholesterol: 53 mg
Fiber: 0
Calcium: 44 mg

To balance your meal, add: Southwestern Corn Salad*,
fruit of choice

Flounder Parmesan

*Try this easy-to-prepare dish when you want a light
and tasty meal.*

cooking spray
1 pound flounder (or other white fish, as desired)
1 cup buttermilk
½ cup Parmesan cheese
1 teaspoon lemon juice
1 tablespoon onion, chopped
½ teaspoon salt
⅛ teaspoon hot pepper sauce
⅛ teaspoon paprika
1 tablespoon fresh parsley, chopped

Preheat the oven to 350 degrees F. Spray a 12-by-8-by-2-inch baking pan with the cooking spray.

Place the fish in the prepared pan. In a small bowl, combine the buttermilk, Parmesan cheese, lemon juice, onion, salt, and pepper sauce. Spread the mixture over the fish. Sprinkle it with the paprika. Bake it for 25 to 30 minutes or until the fish flakes easily with a fork. Garnish it with the parsley before serving.

Makes 4 servings.

Calories per serving: 187
Protein: 29 g
Carbohydrates: 4 g
Fat: 6 g
Cholesterol: 66 mg
Fiber: 0
Calcium: 266 mg

To balance your meal, add: yellow rice, tossed green salad

Baked Fish Supreme

This is a terrific dish for calorie-conscious family members.

cooking spray
1 tablespoon margarine or butter
1 tablespoon onion, chopped
½ cup fresh mushrooms, chopped
½ cup dry white wine
1¼ pounds white fish fillets
dash each salt and black pepper
3 tablespoons bread crumbs
1 tablespoon fresh parsley, chopped

Preheat the oven to 425 degrees F. Spray the baking dish with the cooking spray.

In a medium skillet, heat the margarine or butter over medium heat. Add the onion. Sauté until it's translucent. Add the mushrooms; cook them 1 minute more. Add the wine, and boil it for 1 minute.

Place the fish in the prepared baking dish. Season it with the salt and black pepper. Pour the wine mixture over the fish. Sprinkle it with the bread crumbs. Bake it for 15 to 20 minutes until the fish is cooked and golden brown. Garnish it with the parsley before serving.

Makes 4 servings.

Calories per serving: 184
Protein: 25 g
Carbohydrates: 5 g
Fat: 5 g
Cholesterol: 70 mg
Fiber: 0
Calcium: 38 mg

To balance your meal, add: Spinach and Wild Rice*,
Angel Food Cake and Strawberries*

Southwestern Salmon

*Try a tangy topping the next time you make salmon.
You'll be surprised at how flavorful the meal can be.*

4 salmon fillets (approximately 3 ounces each), with the
   skin removed
salt and black pepper to taste
cooking spray
1 (10-ounce) can diced tomatoes with green chiles, well
   drained
¼ cup light mayonnaise

Season the salmon with the salt and black pepper. Spray a large
skillet with the cooking spray. Heat it to medium.
   Combine the tomatoes and mayonnaise in a medium bowl.
Coat both sides of the salmon with the tomato mixture and place
it in the skillet. Add the remaining tomato mixture to the pan and
cover it. Cook the fillets for 3 to 5 minutes on each side or until
they're done. (Cooking time will vary, depending on the thickness
of the fillets.) The fillets are done when they flake easily with a
fork when poked.

Makes 4 servings.

Calories per serving: 195
Protein: 18 g
Carbohydrates: 6 g
Fat: 10 g
Cholesterol: 53 mg
Fiber: 1 g
Calcium: 22 mg

To balance your meal, add: Zucchini Cornbread Squares,
cole slaw*

Dinner-in-a-Dish

*One-dish meals speak for themselves. They're easy
for Mom and favorites of families.*

1 tablespoon oil
1 green pepper, sliced
1 medium onion, chopped
1 pound lean ground beef
1 teaspoon salt
¼ teaspoon black pepper
2 eggs
2 cups corn niblets, fresh or frozen
1 (14.5-ounce) can diced tomatoes, drained
½ cup dry bread crumbs

Preheat the oven to 375 degrees F.

Heat the oil in a large skillet over medium heat. Add the green pepper and onion. Sauté them for 3 minutes. Add the beef, salt, and black pepper. Remove the mixture from the heat. Stir in the eggs and mix well.

Layer half of the corn in the bottom of a 2-quart baking dish, then half of the beef mixture, then a layer of tomatoes. Repeat with another layer of corn, beef mixture, and tomatoes. Cover this with bread crumbs. Bake it for 30 minutes until it's cooked throughout.

Makes 6 servings.

Calories per serving: 297
Protein: 22 g
Carbohydrates: 28 g
Fat: 11 g
Cholesterol: 90 mg
Fiber: 3 g
Calcium: 87 mg

*To balance your meal, add:
lettuce wedge salad,
Oatmeal Cookie Sandwich**

Beef Casserole

This all-in-one meat, vegetable, and starch dish is hearty, delicious, and well received.

1 pound lean ground beef
1 small onion, chopped
1 (15-ounce) can cut green beans
1 (10¾-ounce) can undiluted tomato soup
cooking spray
2 cups prepared mashed potatoes (do not make mashed potatoes too thin). Instant potatoes can be used.

Preheat the oven to 350 degrees F. In a large skillet, brown the ground beef and the onions until the onions are tender. Add the green beans and tomato soup.

Spray a 2-quart casserole dish with the cooking spray. Pour the meat mixture into the casserole dish and cover it with spoonfuls of the mashed potatoes. Bake the casserole for approximately 15 minutes or until it is bubbly.

Makes 6 servings.

Calories per serving: 258
Protein: 19 g
Carbohydrates: 22 g
Fat: 11 g
Cholesterol: 30 mg
Fiber: 3 g
Calcium: 58 mg

To balance your meal, add: Orange Glazed Carrots*, sliced strawberries with whipped topping

Steak and Veggies in Foil

*This original one-dish meal is a classic from way back.
Bring it back home to your family again. Try it with
the suggested veggies or add your own variations.*

½ pound lean beef round steak
½ packet onion soup mix
2 medium carrots
1 stalk celery
2 medium new potatoes

Preheat the oven to 450 degrees F. Place the steak in the center of a large piece of heavy-duty aluminum foil. Sprinkle the soup mix over the top of the meat. Cut up the vegetables and place them on top of the meat. Close the foil tightly. Set the package on a cookie sheet.

Bake it for 1 hour or until it's done. If you choose to cook on a grill, place the foil directly on the rack and grill it until it's done.

Makes 2 servings.

Calories per serving: 266
Protein: 31 g
Carbohydrates: 23 g
Fat: 5 g
Cholesterol: 71 mg
Fiber: 5 g
Calcium: 50 mg

To balance your meal, add: Freezer Slaw,
Apple Cinnamon Crisp**

Baked Pork and Sweet Potatoes

This dish is tasty and easy to prepare.

2 sweet potatoes
2 tablespoons lemon juice
4 boneless loin pork chops, 3 ounces each
4 slices pineapple, packed in juice
8 whole cloves
8 prunes, pitted, dried
½ cup pineapple juice

Peel the sweet potatoes. Cut them in half lengthwise and rub them with the lemon juice.

In a large skillet, brown the pork chops over medium heat. Place the potatoes cut side down on each pork chop. Top each one with a pineapple slice. Insert the cloves inside each pitted prune and arrange the prunes around the pork chops. Pour the pineapple juice over the entire mixture and cover. Cook this over low heat for 45 minutes.

Makes 4 servings.

Calories per serving: 290
Protein: 21 g
Carbohydrates: 36 g
Fat: 7 g
Cholesterol: 49 mg
Fiber: 4 g
Calcium: 53 mg

*To balance your meal, add: lemon-buttered broccoli,
fruit sherbet*

Company Chicken

A great recipe for entertaining!

1 pound chicken breasts, skinless, boneless
1 tablespoon margarine or butter
16 small white onions, peeled
½ teaspoon salt
⅛ teaspoon black pepper
¼ teaspoon thyme
1½ teaspoons paprika
¾ cup beer
¼ cup tomato sauce
1 bay leaf
¼ cup half-and-half

In a large skillet, brown the chicken in the margarine or butter. Add the onions and cook until they're tender. Add the remaining ingredients, except the half and half. Bring everything to a boil. Cover and simmer it for 30 minutes. Stir in the half-and-half until heated. Serve immediately.

Makes 4 servings.

Calories per serving: 299
Protein: 27 g
Carbohydrates: 28 g
Fat: 8 g
Cholesterol: 73 mg
Fiber: 4 g
Calcium: 87 mg

To balance your meal, add: spanish rice, tossed green salad

Skillet Parmesan Chicken and Rice Dinner

Try various types of pasta as a substitute for the rice.

1 tablespoon olive oil
½ cup onion, chopped
2 garlic cloves, minced
½ teaspoon thyme
4 chicken breasts, boneless, skinless
½ cup dry white wine
1 cup instant rice, uncooked
1 (14-ounce) can chicken broth
2 tablespoons Parmesan cheese, grated

Heat the oil in a skillet. Add the onion, garlic, and thyme. Sauté for 2 minutes until the onion is tender. Add the chicken. Cook it for 3 to 4 minutes on each side until the chicken is lightly browned.

Add the wine. Cook everything about 2 minutes until most of the wine is absorbed. Add the rice and broth. Bring it to a boil, reduce the heat, then simmer it for 10 minutes until the rice is fluffy and the liquid is absorbed. Sprinkle it with Parmesan cheese.

Makes 4 servings.

Calories per serving: 295
Protein: 27 g
Carbohydrates: 20 g
Fat: 9 g
Cholesterol: 67 mg
Fiber: 1 g
Calcium: 73 mg

To balance your meal, add: Oriental Spinach*

Pesto Skillet Chicken

Add some pasta and you're good to go.

1 tablespoon olive oil
4 chicken breasts, skinless, boneless
1 zucchini squash, sliced
1 yellow squash, sliced
2 tablespoons prepared pesto
2 tablespoons Parmesan cheese, grated

Heat the oil in a large skillet. Cook the chicken until it's browned on one side, about 3 minutes, then turn it to cook the other side. Add the zucchini and yellow squash to the skillet. Cook the vegetables another 3 to 4 minutes until the chicken is no longer pink inside and the squash is tender. Spread the pesto over the chicken. Sprinkle it with the Parmesan cheese before serving.

Makes 4 servings.

Calories per serving: 215
Protein: 26 g
Carbohydrates: 3 g
Fat: 10 g
Cholesterol: 67 mg
Fiber: 1 g
Calcium: 120 mg

To balance your meal, add: Mashed Potatoes (or Not)*,
caesar salad

Southwest Chicken Skillet

The great taste of the Southwest can satisfy any hungry family.

4 chicken breasts (about 4 ounces each), boneless,
  skinless
1 teaspoon chili powder
1 teaspoon cumin
salt and black pepper to taste
2 teaspoons vegetable oil
2 cloves garlic, chopped
½ cup prepared salsa
1 tablespoon spicy mustard
½ cup Monterey Jack cheese, shredded

Sprinkle the chicken with the chili powder, cumin, salt, and black pepper.

Heat the oil and garlic in a large skillet over medium heat. Add the chicken breasts. Cook them until they're browned, about 3 minutes on each side.

In a small bowl, combine the salsa and mustard. Add them to the skillet. Cook the chicken for an additional 5 to 7 minutes until it is cooked throughout and is no longer pink in the center. Sprinkle it with the shredded cheese. Heat the skillet until the cheese melts. Serve it immediately.

Makes 4 servings.

Calories per serving: 215
Protein: 27 g
Carbohydrates: 3 g
Fat: 10 g
Cholesterol: 75 mg
Fiber: 1 g
Calcium: 140 mg

To balance your meal, add: Broccoli Rice*, orange sherbet

Chicken Taco Skillet

*A tasty one-dish fast-food meal that can be made quickly
and easily. Get the kids to help, too.*

1 teaspoon vegetable oil
4 chicken breasts, boneless, skinless, cut into 1-inch
    pieces
1 (16-ounce) bag frozen broccoli, corn, and red peppers
1 (15-ounce) can black beans, drained
1 cup prepared salsa
1½ cups tortilla chips, crushed
¾ cup low-fat cheddar cheese, shredded

Heat the oil in a large skillet. Add the chicken and cook it until it's
browned and no longer pink inside.

Add the frozen vegetables, beans, and salsa to the skillet.
Cover and simmer it on low for 8 to 10 minutes or until the
vegetables are tender-crisp.

Top the mixture with the tortilla chips and cheese. Heat it 1 to
2 minutes more, until the cheese is slightly melted.

Makes 6 servings.

Calories per serving: 248
Protein: 23 g
Carbohydrates: 26 g
Fat: 6 g
Cholesterol: 35 mg
Fiber: 7 g
Calcium: 130 mg

*To balance your meal, add: lettuce and tomato salad,
pineapple slices*

Chicken and Brown Rice Pilaf

*By using chicken strips for this recipe, it will
cook faster, and the kids may enjoy it more.
Also, you can substitute broccoli or other
vegetable blends for the vegetables in this dish.*

1 teaspoon vegetable oil
4 chicken breasts, cut into strips (about 4 ounces each),
    boneless, skinless
1 (10½-ounce) can chicken broth
½ cup water
1 cup mushrooms, fresh or canned, sliced
1 small onion, chopped
1 cup frozen peas
1½ cups instant brown rice, uncooked

In a large skillet, heat the oil. Add the chicken and cook it on both
sides until it's lightly browned and no longer pink inside. Remove
it from the skillet and set it aside.

Add the chicken broth and water. Heat this to a boil. Stir in the
mushrooms, onion, peas, and rice. Reduce the heat to a simmer.
Return the chicken to the skillet. Cover and cook it for about 5 to
8 minutes more, until the rice is thoroughly cooked.

Makes 6 servings.

Calories per serving: 223
Protein: 21 g
Carbohydrates: 24 g
Fat: 4 g
Cholesterol: 42 mg
Fiber: 3 g
Calcium: 23 mg

To balance your meal, add: Fruity Acorn Squash*

Lemon Chicken and Broccoli

This dish is light, delicious, and great for family meals or entertaining.

4 chicken breasts (4 ounces each), boneless, skinless
¼ cup lemon juice
2 teaspoons vegetable oil
2 garlic cloves, minced
2 cups broccoli florets, fresh or frozen
1 (14-ounce) can chicken broth

Combine the chicken breasts and lemon juice in a resealable plastic bag. Marinate them in the refrigerator for 30 minutes to 1 hour.

Drain the chicken, reserving the marinade. Heat the oil and garlic in a large skillet over medium heat. Add the chicken. Cook until it's browned, about 3 minutes on each side.

Reduce the heat to low. Add the marinade, broccoli, and broth. Simmer this for about 15 to 20 minutes until the chicken is cooked throughout and the broccoli is tender.

Makes 4 servings.

Calories per serving: 174
Protein: 24 g
Carbohydrates: 3 g
Fat: 7 g
Cholesterol: 65 mg
Fiber: 1 g
Calcium: 32 mg

To balance your meal, add: baked potato, Oatmeal Cookie Sandwich*

Chicken Tortellini Primavera

White, creamy pasta sauce is typically higher in fat than red pasta sauces. If you want to reduce the amount of fat in this dish, substitute a red sauce for the Alfredo.

    1 (9-ounce) package refrigerated cheese tortellini
    2 teaspoons vegetable oil
    4 chicken breasts, boneless, skinless, cut into bite-sized
        chunks
    1 red pepper, chopped
    1 onion, chopped
    ½ of a (10-ounce) jar Alfredo sauce
    ½ cup frozen peas

Cook the tortellini according to the package directions.

In a large skillet, heat the oil. Add the chicken and stir-fry until it's lightly browned and cooked throughout, about 5 minutes. Remove the chicken and set it aside.

Add the red pepper and onion to the skillet. Cook until they're tender. Return the chicken to the skillet. Add the Alfredo sauce, tortellini, and peas. Cook until everything is heated throughout. Serve immediately.

Makes 4 servings.

Calories per serving: 420
Protein: 25 g
Carbohydrates: 37 g
Fat: 13 g
Cholesterol: 96 mg
Fiber: 2 g
Calcium: 223 mg

*To balance your meal, add: tossed green salad,
French bread, cantaloupe wedge*

Spinach Lasagna

*We call this "lazy lasagna" because you don't have to
cook the lasagna noodles in advance. The microwave's
time-saving steps help to create this meatless main dish.*

½ teaspoon margarine or butter
½ cup onion, chopped
1 clove garlic, minced
1 (14½-ounce) can diced tomatoes
½ teaspoon oregano
1 teaspoon basil
1 teaspoon brown sugar
¼ cup tomato paste
1 tablespoon Parmesan cheese, grated
1 cup low-fat cottage cheese
1 (10-ounce) package frozen spinach, thawed and drained
3 uncooked lasagna noodles
¾ cup mozzarella cheese, shredded

In a medium glass bowl, microwave the margarine or butter until
it's melted. Stir in the onion and garlic. Cover the bowl and
microwave it on medium-high for 1 minute. Add the undrained
tomatoes, spices, brown sugar, and tomato paste. Cover the bowl
with a paper towel and microwave it on high for 10 minutes. Stir
in the Parmesan cheese and set the bowl aside.

In a separate bowl, mix the cottage cheese and spinach.
Assemble the lasagna in a 9-by-5-by-2-inch glass loaf pan, beginning with ¼ cup of the sauce mixture; the uncooked noodles, bro-
ken into thirds; the cheese-spinach mixture; half of the mozzarella
cheese; and half of the remaining sauce. Repeat with the noodles,
cheese-spinach mixture, and sauce, and top the lasagna with the
remaining mozzarella cheese. Cover the pan with plastic wrap.
Microwave it on high for 6 minutes; then on medium-high for 15
minutes. Let it stand for 15 minutes before serving.

Makes 4 servings.

Calories per serving: 236
Protein: 19 g
Carbohydrates: 28 g
Fat: 6 g
Cholesterol: 16 mg
Fiber: 6 g
Calcium: 336 mg

To balance your meal, add: mixed green salad,
Oatmeal Cookie Sandwich*

Ravioli Lasagna

You can't get much easier than this when it comes to lasagna.
Keep this dish in mind for a quick meal on a busy day.

> 1 (26-ounce) jar pasta sauce, any variety
> 1 cup water
> 1 (18-ounce) package refrigerated ravioli, any variety
> 2 cups mozzarella cheese, shredded

Preheat the oven to 375 degrees F. Combine the pasta sauce and water in a large bowl.

Put half of the sauce in a 9-by-13-inch baking pan. Top it with half of the ravioli and half of the mozzarella cheese. Repeat with the ravioli, then put the remaining sauce on top. Cover it with foil. Bake it for 1 hour. Remove the foil and top the lasagna with the remaining cheese. Bake it for an additional 10 minutes.

Makes 8 servings.

Calories per serving: 276
Protein: 15 g
Carbohydrates: 29 g
Fat: 11 g
Cholesterol: 41 mg
Fiber: 3 g
Calcium: 291 mg

To balance your meal, add: steamed green beans,
watermelon balls

Quick Tamale Casserole

This meal can be put together on a night when nothing else is available, as long as you have a stocked pantry. Just open the cans, and dinner is ready in a flash.

1 (13½-ounce) can tamales
1 (15-ounce) can chili with beans
1 small onion, finely chopped
1 (3-ounce) can ripe olives, sliced
½ cup low-fat cheddar cheese, shredded, divided

Preheat the oven to 350 degrees F.

Cut the tamales into 2-inch pieces. Add the chili, onion, and olives.

Put the mixture into a 2-quart casserole dish. Sprinkle it with ¼ cup of the cheese. Bake it for 30 minutes. Sprinkle it with the remaining cheese; bake it for 5 more minutes.

Makes 8 servings.

Calories per serving: 196
Protein: 8 g
Carbohydrates: 17 g
Fat: 11 g
Cholesterol: 17 mg
Fiber: 3 g
Calcium: 82 mg

To balance your meal, add: Freezer Slaw*, fruit of choice

Tuna Noodle Casserole

This old classic favorite is always a hit with the family. You can also prepare it in advance, and bake it later to save time.

> cooking spray
> 3 ounces thin egg noodles or bowtie macaroni
>   (3 cups cooked)
> 1 (7-ounce) can water-packed tuna, drained, or
>   1 (5-ounce) package flavor-fresh tuna
> 1 (10¾-ounce) can cream of mushroom soup
> ½ cup low-fat milk
> 1 (15-ounce) can green peas, drained, or 1½ cups frozen
>   green peas
> 2 eggs, hard-boiled, chopped (optional)
> ½ cup Parmesan cheese, grated

Preheat the oven to 350 degrees F. Spray a 1½-quart casserole dish with the cooking spray.

Prepare the noodles according to the package directions. Drain them.

In the prepared casserole dish, combine the drained noodles, tuna, mushroom soup, and milk. Mix them well. Stir in the peas and eggs, if desired. Sprinkle the cheese over the top. Bake it for 30 to 40 minutes or until the sauce is bubbly and the top is lightly browned.

Makes 8 servings.

Calories per serving: 190
Protein: 14 g
Carbohydrates: 21 g
Fat: 6 g
Cholesterol: 30 mg
Fiber: 2 g
Calcium: 114 mg

4-WAY TUNA NOODLE CASSEROLE VARIATIONS

Follow the basic recipe, then try the following variations to suit your family's tastes.

#1: For additional color, add pimentos.

#2: For more mushroom flavor, add a small can of mushroom stems or pieces.

#3: For variety in the vegetables, substitute broccoli or green beans for green peas.

#4: For a crunchier topping, combine bread crumbs or crushed potato chips with grated cheese.

To balance your meal, add: applesauce cups

Applesauce Raisin Muffins

Opt for healthful muffins instead of doughnuts for a quick breakfast. Make these over the weekend and freeze them so that they are always available. Try as mini-muffins, too.

cooking spray
1½ cups uncooked oats
1½ cups all-purpose flour
¾ teaspoon ground cinnamon
¼ teaspoon ground nutmeg
1 teaspoon baking powder
¾ teaspoon baking soda
1 cup unsweetened applesauce
½ cup low-fat milk
½ cup brown sugar, firmly packed
2 tablespoons vegetable oil
1 egg white
½ cup raisins

Topping:
1 tablespoon brown sugar
¼ teaspoon ground cinnamon
⅛ teaspoon ground nutmeg
1 tablespoon margarine or butter, melted

Preheat the oven to 400 degrees F. Spray the muffin pan, or a mini-muffin pan, with the cooking spray.

In a large bowl, combine all of the muffin ingredients. Fill the muffin pans three-quarters full. Combine the topping ingredients and sprinkle them over the muffin batter.

Bake the muffins for 20 minutes or until they're golden brown. Serve them warm or cool and freeze some for later.

Makes 12 muffins or 36 mini-muffins.

Calories per serving: 193
Protein: 4 g
Carbohydrates: 38 g
Fat: 4 g
Cholesterol: 2 mg
Fiber: 2 g
Calcium: 53 mg

To balance your meal, add: Berry Banana Smoothie*

Turkey Chili

Make a double batch of this chili, part of it for tonight's
dinner, then freeze the rest for later in the month.
Ground chicken could be substituted for turkey, if desired.

2 teaspoons vegetable oil
1 small onion, chopped
$\frac{1}{2}$ cup green pepper, chopped
$\frac{1}{2}$ pound lean ground turkey
1 garlic clove, minced
1 tablespoon chili powder
1 teaspoon ground cumin
1 ($14\frac{1}{2}$-ounce) can diced tomatoes
1 ($15\frac{1}{2}$-ounce) can kidney, white, or great northern beans,
    drained and rinsed

Heat the oil in a medium skillet. Add the onion and pepper. Cook until they're tender-crisp, about 3 to 4 minutes. Remove them from the skillet. Set them aside.

Add the ground turkey, garlic, chili powder, and cumin to the skillet. Heat these until the turkey is cooked through, about 3 to 4 minutes.

Stir in the tomatoes and beans. Bring the mixture to a boil, then reduce the heat to a simmer. Stir in the onion and green pepper. Cover and heat everything for an additional 10 minutes.

Makes 4 servings.

Calories per serving: 299
Protein: 18 g
Carbohydrates: 38 g
Fat: 8 g
Cholesterol: 47 mg
Fiber: 9 g
Calcium: 97 mg

To balance your meal, add: Hearty Sweet and
Sour Slaw*, crackers

Our Favorite Chili

This chili has real homemade flavor, and it freezes well, too.
Package the leftovers in small freezer bags for busy days.

1½ pounds lean ground beef
½ cup onion, chopped
1 garlic clove, minced
2 (15½-ounce) cans dark red kidney beans
2 (14½-ounce) cans diced tomatoes
1 (8-ounce) can tomato paste
1-ounce package chili seasoning mix
1 teaspoon prepared horseradish
1 teaspoon hot sauce

In a large skillet, brown the ground beef, onion, and garlic. Add the undrained beans, tomatoes, tomato paste, and chili mix. Simmer everything for 5 minutes. Add the remaining ingredients. Simmer the chili for another 30 to 40 minutes.

Makes 8 servings.

Calories per serving: 294
Protein: 26 g
Carbohydrates: 30 g
Fat: 8 g
Cholesterol: 31 mg
Fiber: 9 g
Calcium: 88 mg

To balance your meal, add: fresh sliced vegetables,
oyster crackers

Basic Chicken or Beef Broth

It's not very difficult to make your own broth by simmering
a chicken or meat bones with vegetables and seasonings.
You can even add some of the shredded, cooked chicken
back into the broth for a "meatier" broth. Use it instead of
canned broth or bouillon cubes in soups and other recipes.

> 6 cups cold water
> 2–3 pounds chicken parts or 2–3 pounds beef bones
> 1 onion, chopped
> 2–3 carrots, chopped
> 2–3 stalks celery, chopped
> 1 bay leaf
> black pepper, parsley, and thyme to taste

In a large Dutch oven or stockpot, combine all of the ingredients.
Simmer them for 1 to 2 hours. Strain the broth, chill it, and skim
off the fat. The stock may be stored in the refrigerator for several
days or in the freezer for up to 6 months. If you freeze your stock
in ice cube trays and store the frozen cubes in freezer bags, you
will always have a homemade broth available in small amounts.

Makes 4 servings.

Calories per serving (broth only, without added chicken): 29
Protein: 1 g
Carbohydrates: 7 g
Fat: 0
Cholesterol: 0
Fiber: 2 g
Calcium: 23 mg

Creamy Tomato Soup

*This soup is a staple in any home, but it tastes
better when it's homemade.*

1 (28-ounce) can whole tomatoes in juice
1 tablespoon oil
1 onion, chopped
1 (14½-ounce) can chicken broth
¼ cup dry white wine
1 teaspoon brown sugar
½ teaspoon thyme
1 cup low-fat milk
½ cup mozzarella cheese, shredded

In a medium bowl, mash the tomatoes into small pieces with a
fork or a potato masher.

Heat the oil in a large saucepan over medium-low heat. Add the
onion. Cook it for 2 to 3 minutes until it's tender. Add the tomatoes,
broth, wine, brown sugar, and thyme. Heat the mixture to boiling.
Reduce the heat to low and simmer everything for 5 minutes.

Taking about 1 cup at a time, put the mixture into a blender
and blend until it's smooth. Return it to the saucepan. Add the
milk and heat thoroughly.

To serve, pour the soup into bowls and top each one with the
mozzarella cheese.

Makes 6 servings.

Calories per serving: 135
Protein: 9 g
Carbohydrates: 12 g
Fat: 6 g
Cholesterol: 9 mg
Fiber: 2 g
Calcium: 180 mg

To balance your meal, add: Crunchy Tuna Pita Pockets*, apple

Mom's Potato Soup

Try using our homemade chicken broth for a nice,
but not salty, flavor.

1 tablespoon margarine or butter
3 medium potatoes, peeled and sliced
1 medium onion, chopped
1 cup celery, chopped
2 cups Basic Chicken Broth (or other preferred broth)
1 bay leaf
¼ teaspoon salt
1 cup low-fat milk
⅛ teaspoon paprika
1 tablespoon parsley, fresh, chopped

In a large Dutch oven or a stockpot, heat the margarine or butter. Sauté the potatoes, onion, and celery until translucent. Add the chicken broth to cover the potatoes. Add the bay leaf. Simmer the vegetables until they're tender, about 15 minutes. Remove the bay leaf and add the salt.

Put the mixture, about 1 cup at a time, in a blender or a food processor. Blend until it's smooth. Return the mixture to the stockpot. Add the milk and heat thoroughly. Garnish the soup with the paprika and parsley before serving it.

Makes 5 servings.

Calories per serving: 170
Protein: 8 g
Carbohydrates: 26 g
Fat: 4 g
Cholesterol: 6 mg
Fiber: 3 g
Calcium: 86 mg

To balance your meal, add: Fresh Fruit Pizza*

5-Way Cream Soup

*Start with the cream soup base and add your
favorite ingredients.*

Cream Soup Base

1 tablespoon margarine or butter
¼ cup green onions, chopped
2 tablespoons flour
1½ cups chicken broth (you can use our homemade recipe
   or canned)
1½ cups low-fat milk
½ teaspoon salt (omit if you are using canned broth with
   sodium)
⅛ teaspoon black pepper

In a large saucepan, melt the margarine or butter and sauté the
onion. Add the flour and cook until it's bubbly. Add the broth and
blend it well. Add the remaining ingredients and cook them over
medium heat until the mixture thickens, stirring constantly. Simmer it for 5 minutes.

Makes 4 servings.

Calories per serving: 120
Protein: 8 g
Carbohydrates: 9 g
Fat: 6 g
Cholesterol: 12 mg
Fiber: 0
Calcium: 109 mg

Cream of Corn Soup

Cut the kernels from three ears of corn and add them to the soup base. Add 2 tablespoons of chopped green pepper. Simmer it for 10 minutes.

Calories per serving: 174
Protein: 9 g
Carbohydrates: 20 g
Fat: 6 g
Cholesterol: 12 mg
Fiber: 1 g
Calcium: 109 mg

Cream of Broccoli Soup

Cook 1½ cups of coarsely chopped broccoli until it's tender. Add it to the soup base and simmer it for 5 minutes.

Calories per serving: 129
Protein: 8 g
Carbohydrates: 11 g
Fat: 6 g
Cholesterol: 12 mg
Fiber: 1 g
Calcium: 125 mg

Cream of Spinach Soup

Thaw half of a 10-ounce package of chopped spinach, and drain the excess liquid. Add it to the soup base with a dash of nutmeg. Simmer it for 10 minutes.

Calories per serving: 128
Protein: 9 g
Carbohydrates: 10 g
Fat: 6 g
Cholesterol: 12 mg
Fiber: 1 g
Calcium: 146 mg

Cream of Chicken Soup

Steam ½ cup of chopped celery until it's tender. Add the celery, 1 cup of chopped, cooked chicken, and 1 tablespoon of chopped pimento to the soup base. Simmer it for 10 minutes.

Calories per serving: 194
Protein: 21 g
Carbohydrates: 10 g
Fat: 7 g
Cholesterol: 48 mg
Fiber: 1 g
Calcium: 121 mg

Easy Carrot Bisque

Add 1 (4½-ounce) jar each of strained baby food squash, carrots, and applesauce to the soup base. Add ⅛ teaspoon of curry powder. Serve it hot or cold, sprinkled with nutmeg.

Calories per serving: 150
Protein: 8 g
Carbohydrates: 16 g
Fat: 6 g
Cholesterol: 12 mg
Fiber: 2 g
Calcium: 125 mg

White Chicken Chili

*Here's a nice hearty change from the beef–tomato base chili.
Make a large batch for Sunday dinner, and freeze a
batch for a busy night later in the month.*

1 medium onion, finely chopped
1 (4-ounce) jar green chilies, drained, chopped
2 teaspoons ground cumin
1 teaspoon chili powder
½ teaspoon salt
2 (16-ounce) cans navy or great northern beans
2 cups chicken breast, about 2 breasts, cooked, chopped
1 (14½-ounce) can low-fat chicken broth (approximately
    3½ cups)

In a large saucepan or a Dutch oven, combine all of the ingredients. Bring them to a boil, then reduce the heat to low. Simmer the chili for 1½ to 2 hours or until it's thickened. Garnish it with the sour cream or shredded cheese, as desired.

Makes 6 servings.

Calories per serving: 185
Protein: 15 g
Carbohydrates: 26 g
Fat: 3 g
Cholesterol: 17 mg
Fiber: 9 g
Calcium: 113 mg

*To balance your meal, add: crispy rolls,
fresh fruit of choice*

Taco Soup

*This soup serves as a great start to a meal or
as a meal in itself.*

1 pound very lean ground beef
1 tablespoon vegetable or olive oil
1 medium onion, chopped
1 package ranch-flavored dressing mix
1 package taco seasoning mix
1 (15-ounce) can black beans, undrained
1 (15-ounce) can red chili, kidney, or red beans, undrained
1 (15-ounce) can whole kernel corn, undrained
1 (15-ounce) can stewed tomatoes, undrained
1 (15-ounce) can stewed tomatoes, Mexican seasoned
1 cup water

In a large saucepan or a Dutch oven, brown the ground beef in the
oil. Add the onions and cook until the onions are translucent. Stir
in all of the remaining ingredients. Bring everything to a rolling
boil. Reduce the heat to a simmer and cook it for 1 hour or until
all the ingredients are blended thoroughly.

Makes 8 servings (approximately 1½ cups per serving).

Calories per serving: 228
Protein: 16 g
Carbohydrates: 27 g
Fat: 6 g
Cholesterol: 16 mg
Fiber: 8 g
Calcium: 39 mg

To balance your meal, add: Zucchini Cornbread Squares,
fresh melon balls*

Easy Baked Spaghetti

*This is a great way to serve spaghetti for children. It can
be cut in squares and is much easier to eat.*

1½ pounds lean ground beef, turkey, or chicken
1 (26-ounce jar) spaghetti sauce
8 ounces uncooked angel hair pasta
¾ cup cheddar cheese, shredded
¾ cup Monterey Jack cheese, shredded

Preheat the oven to 350 degrees F. In a large skillet, brown the
ground beef. Drain the fat from the beef, then add the spaghetti
sauce to the skillet.

Prepare the pasta according to the package directions. Cook
until it's firm and slightly stiff. Drain it.

Cover the bottom of a 13-by-9-by-2-inch baking dish with a
layer of meat sauce. Add a layer of spaghetti and then half of the
two cheeses; repeat with a layer of spaghetti, ending with the meat
sauce. Bake it for 30 minutes. Top the casserole with the other half
of the cheeses; return the casserole to the oven and continue to
cook it until the cheese is melted and bubbly, about 5 minutes
more. Cool it slightly. Cut it into squares before serving.

Makes 12 servings.

Calories per serving: 249
Protein: 20 g
Carbohydrates: 18 g
Fat: 10 g
Cholesterol: 31 mg
Fiber: 2 g
Calcium: 135 mg

To balance your meal, add:
Dilled Green Beans*, garlic toast

Cheesy Chicken and Rice Stuffed Peppers

Here's a great use for leftover cooked chicken. You can also prepare this dish in advance and cook it just in time for dinner.

cooking spray
1 tablespoon margarine or butter
1 small onion, finely chopped
1 (10¾-ounce) can cream of mushroom soup
1 cup water
1 dry packet onion soup mix
2 cups chicken, cooked, diced
3 cups cooked rice, white or brown
5 large sweet green peppers
salt and black pepper to taste
1 cup mozzarella cheese, shredded

Preheat the oven to 350 degrees F. Spray a large shallow baking or roasting pan with the cooking spray.

In a large saucepan, melt the margarine or butter. Add the onion and cook until it's tender, about 3 minutes. Add the soup, water, and onion soup mix. Heat this mixture on medium-high heat until it's boiling. Add the chicken and the rice. Once it's thoroughly heated, remove it from the heat.

Cut the peppers in half lengthwise, removing the seeds and membranes. Place the peppers in the prepared baking dish. Divide the chicken mixture evenly among the 10 pepper halves. Sprinkle them with the salt and black pepper, as desired. Cover them loosely with aluminum foil.

(If you choose to bake them later, cover the dish securely and place it in the refrigerator. Follow the remaining directions when you're ready to bake and serve the peppers.)

(continued)

Cheesy Chicken and Rice Stuffed Peppers (continued)

Bake the peppers for 30 to 45 minutes or until they are tender. Remove the foil, top them with the shredded cheese, and bake them for an additional 5 minutes.

Makes 10 servings.

Calories per serving: 222
Protein: 16 g
Carbohydrates: 23 g
Fat: 7 g
Cholesterol: 37 mg
Fiber: 2 g
Calcium: 105 mg

To balance your meal, add: lettuce wedge with dressing, fruit cocktail cup

Leftover Fried Rice

This one-dish meal works great with leftovers, such as chicken breasts, beef, or shrimp.

1 tablespoon oil
¼ cup green onions, chopped
1 clove garlic, minced
1 egg, beaten
½ cup carrots, chopped or shredded
½ cup peas, frozen
2 cooked leftover chicken breasts, cut up
4 cups rice, cooked, cold
1 tablespoon soy sauce

Place the skillet over medium heat. Add the oil, onions, and garlic. Stir-fry these for about 2 minutes or until the onion is tender. Pour in the beaten egg to scramble it. Remove it and set it aside.

Add the carrots, peas, and chicken to the skillet. Add the rice and toss. Add the soy sauce and scrambled egg and toss to mix everything well.

Makes 8 servings.

Calories per serving: 188
Protein: 10 g
Carbohydrates: 28 g
Fat: 3 g
Cholesterol: 41 mg
Fiber: 1 g
Calcium: 11 mg

To balance your meal, add: egg roll, mandarin oranges

Chicken Tetrazzini

This recipe can easily be doubled and frozen.

3 tablespoons onion, chopped
2 teaspoons margarine or butter
2 (10¾ ounce) cans fat-free cream of mushroom soup
½ cup water
½ cup low-fat cheddar cheese, shredded
2 tablespoons sherry
2 cups chicken, cooked, diced
2 tablespoons pimento, chopped
1 tablespoon parsley, chopped
2 cups vermicelli or very thin spaghetti, cooked

In a saucepan, sauté the onion in the margarine or butter until it's tender. Blend in the soup, water, cheese, and sherry. Heat it until the cheese melts, while stirring. Add the chicken, pimento, parsley, and cooked vermicelli or spaghetti. Transfer the mixture to a casserole dish. (You can prepare this ahead of time and refrigerate or freeze it. If freezing the dish, defrost before heating.) When ready to serve, preheat the oven to 350 degrees F. Heat until bubbly, about 20 to 25 minutes.

Makes 4 servings.

Calories per serving: 298
Protein: 17 g
Carbohydrates: 30 g
Fat: 11 g
Cholesterol: 39 mg
Fiber: 3 g
Calcium: 101 mg

To balance your meal, add: Italian Bread Knots*, tossed salad

Our Favorite Meat Loaf

*Meat loaf has come full circle since the 1950s and is enjoying
popularity even in restaurants as a favorite comfort food.
Not only can you make this ahead of time, but you can
freeze what is left over and use it for sandwiches.*

1 pound lean ground beef or turkey
1 cup (approximately 16) crushed saltine crackers
½ cup onion, chopped
¼ cup green pepper, chopped
½ cup celery, chopped
1 egg, beaten
1 (8½-ounce) can stewed tomatoes, drained
½ teaspoon garlic powder
½ teaspoon salt
¼ teaspoon black pepper

Preheat the oven to 325 degrees F. In a large bowl, combine all of
the ingredients, mixing them lightly. Put them in a 7-by-3-by-2-
inch loaf pan or shape them into a loaf and place this in a baking
dish. Bake the meatloaf 1 to 1½ hours or until it's done completely.

Makes 6 servings.

Calories per serving: 195
Protein: 18 g
Carbohydrates: 10 g
Fat: 9 g
Cholesterol: 63 mg
Fiber: 1 g
Calcium: 40 mg

To balance your meal, add: Baked Potatoes Florentine,
fruit of choice*

Freezer Coleslaw

This easy-to-prepare slaw keeps in the refrigerator for up to one week, or it can be frozen in single portions in freezer bags.

2½ cups cabbage (fresh or packaged), shredded
2 tablespoons carrots, grated
2 tablespoons green pepper, chopped
2 tablespoons onion, chopped
¼ cup vinegar
1 tablespoon water
½ cup sugar
¼ teaspoon celery seed

Soak the vegetables in salted water for 1 hour (add 1 tablespoon of salt to enough water to cover the vegetables). In a large saucepan, combine the vinegar, water, sugar, and celery seed to make a dressing. Boil this for 1 minute and cool it. Drain the salt water from the vegetables, add the dressing, and toss. Refrigerate it for several hours before serving or freeze in single-portion freezer bags for several days.

Makes 4 servings.

Calories per serving: 161
Protein: 1 g
Carbohydrates: 41 g
Fat: 0
Cholesterol: 0
Fiber: 1 g
Calcium: 29 mg

*To balance your meal, add: Roast Beef and
Cheese Deli Wraps**

Hearty Sweet and Sour Slaw

This delicious slaw will keep in the refrigerator for at least a week. It's a great complement to a meal or enhancement to a sandwich.

5 cups cabbage, shredded (may use precut packaged cabbage)
1 medium red bell pepper, chopped
1 onion, chopped
1 cup canned yellow corn, drained
⅓ cup sugar
½ cup rice vinegar
salt and black pepper, to taste
1 tablespoon jalapeno pepper, seeds and veins removed, finely minced (optional)

In a large bowl, toss the cabbage, red pepper, onion, and corn together. In a small bowl combine the sugar and rice vinegar. Sprinkle the cabbage mixture with the salt and pepper, as desired. Add the jalapeno pepper if desired. Pour the vinegar mixture over the cabbage and toss well.

Store the slaw in an airtight container. Refrigerate it for at least two hours before serving.

Makes 10 servings.

Calories per serving: 62
Protein: 1 g
Carbohydrates: 15 g
Fat: 0
Cholesterol: 0
Fiber: 2 g
Calcium: 21 mg

To balance your meal, add: Creamy Chicken Salad*

SIDE DISHES

Mashed Potatoes (or Not)

*Your family might or might not be able to tell the difference,
but they surely will enjoy this new side dish.*

1 teaspoon olive oil
1 small head cauliflower, cut into florets
3 garlic cloves, minced
3 green onions, chopped
⅓ to ½ cup low-fat milk
2 tablespoons light margarine
salt and black pepper to taste

Preheat the oven to 450 degrees F. Toss the oil, cauliflower, and garlic in a baking pan. Bake them for 25 to 30 minutes, stirring frequently, until the cauliflower is browned and softened.

Put the cauliflower in a large bowl. Add the onions, milk (start with ⅓ cup and gradually add more as needed), and margarine. Mash everything with a potato masher until it's the desired consistency. (If preferred, you can use a food processor to mash the cauliflower.) Add the salt and black pepper to taste.

Makes 4 servings.

Calories per serving: 83
Protein: 4 g
Carbohydrates: 11 g
Fat: 3 g
Cholesterol: 1 mg
Fiber: 3 g
Calcium: 60 mg

To balance your meal, add: Choice of 5-Way Chicken Breast,
steamed green beans*

Orange-Glazed Carrots

This tasty dish entices kids of all ages to try it.

cooking spray
1 (16-ounce) package baby carrots
⅓ cup orange marmalade
¼ cup brown sugar, packed
½ teaspoon ground cinnamon
1 teaspoon margarine or butter

Preheat the oven to 450 degrees F. Spray a 2-quart baking dish with the cooking spray. In a medium bowl, toss the carrots with the remaining ingredients. Pour them into the prepared pan. Bake this for 30 minutes or until the carrots are soft, stirring occasionally.

Makes 6 servings.

Calories per serving: 113
Protein: 1 g
Carbohydrates: 27 g
Fat: 1 g
Cholesterol: 1 mg
Fiber: 1 g
Calcium: 34 mg

To balance your meal, add: Crunchy Chicken*,
fresh strawberries

Carrot Fries

*Try a new way to serve carrots. They will soon become
a family favorite.*

> cooking spray
> 4 carrots, peeled and sliced into strips, about 2 to 3 inches
>   long
> 2 teaspoons vegetable oil
> ¼ teaspoon salt

Preheat the oven to 400 degrees F. Spray a baking dish with the
cooking spray. In a medium bowl, toss the carrot strips with the
vegetable oil and the salt. Place them in a baking dish in a single
layer. Bake them 20 to 30 minutes or until they're tender-crisp.

Makes 2 servings.

Calories per serving: 93
Protein: 1 g
Carbohydrates: 12 g
Fat: 5 g
Cholesterol: 0
Fiber: 4 g
Calcium: 33 mg

To balance your meal, add: Pesto Skillet Chicken,
Southwestern Corn Salad**

Sweet Potatoes and Apples

This easy, colorful dish goes well with roast turkey or baked pork chops.

1 sweet potato
1 apple
pinch cinnamon
¼ teaspoon lemon juice
1 teaspoon margarine or butter
1 teaspoon brown sugar
2 tablespoons water

Preheat the oven to 350 degrees F. Cook the sweet potato in the microwave on high until it's nearly done, about 4 minutes. Peel and slice the potato into ½-inch round slices. Cut the apple into wedges, leaving the skin on. In a small greased 1-quart baking dish, alternately layer 1 potato slice with 1 apple wedge. Sprinkle the layers with the remaining ingredients. Bake it for 15 minutes until the apple is soft.

Makes 2 servings.

Calories per serving: 121
Protein: 1 g
Carbohydrates: 26 g
Fat: 2 g
Cholesterol: 2 mg
Fiber: 3 g
Calcium: 21 mg

*To balance your meal, add: Lemon Chicken and Broccoli**

Oven-Baked Eggplant

*This dish is something tasty for the whole
family to enjoy.*

cooking spray
1 small eggplant (about 1 pound)
½ cup light mayonnaise
1 tablespoon onion, minced
¼ teaspoon salt
⅓ cup Italian bread crumbs
⅓ cup Parmesan cheese, grated

Preheat the oven to 425 degrees F. Spray a shallow pan with the cooking spray. Wash the eggplant. Peel and slice it into ¾-inch slices. Set it aside.

Mix the mayonnaise, onion, and salt. Let them stand 5 minutes. Brush both sides of the sliced eggplant with the mayonnaise mixture. Coat the sliced eggplant with the bread crumbs and Parmesan cheese. Place it in the prepared pan. Bake it for 15 to 17 minutes or until it's browned.

Makes 6 servings.

Calories per serving: 135
Protein: 4 g
Carbohydrates: 11 g
Fat: 9 g
Cholesterol: 11 mg
Fiber: 2 g
Calcium: 96 mg

To balance your meal, add: Fettuccine Broccoli Alfredo*

Nutty Broccoli

*Adding pecans to your broccoli creates a new, fun twist
on a plain favorite.*

2 (10-ounce) packages frozen broccoli florets or 3 cups
   fresh broccoli
2 tablespoons margarine or butter
½ package dry onion soup mix
½ cup water chestnuts, drained, chopped
½ cup pecans, chopped

Preheat the oven to 350 degrees F. Heat the frozen broccoli until
it can easily be separated. If you're using fresh broccoli, steam it
for 5 minutes. Place the broccoli in a 1½-quart casserole dish.

In a small saucepan, melt the margarine or butter. Add the soup
mix, water chestnuts, and pecans. Mix them well. Spoon them
over the broccoli. Bake the broccoli for 10 to 15 minutes until it's
heated through.

Makes 6 servings.

Calories per serving: 108
Protein: 4 g
Carbohydrates: 8 g
Fat: 8 g
Cholesterol: 4 mg
Fiber: 4 g
Calcium: 63 mg

To balance your meal, add: Baked Fish Supreme,
French bread*

Fruity Acorn Squash

Bring out the squash for a change of pace.

1 acorn squash (approximately 1 pound)
⅛ teaspoon ground nutmeg
dash salt
2 teaspoons margarine or butter
2 tablespooons apricot preserves
2 tablespoons pecans, chopped

Wash the squash. Pierce it with a knife in two places and place it on a microwavable plate. Cook it on high for 2 minutes. Cut the squash into quarters lengthwise. Remove the seeds and fibers. Turn the squash cut-side up and sprinkle each piece with the nutmeg and a dash of salt, if desired. To each piece, add ½ teaspoon of the margarine or butter, 1½ teaspoons of the preserves, and 1½ teaspoons of the pecans. Cook the squash, covered, on high for 4 minutes or until it is tender. Remove the cover. Let the squash stand for 5 minutes before serving.

Makes 4 servings.

Calories per serving: 110
Protein: 1 g
Carbohydrates: 18 g
Fat: 5 g
Cholesterol: 2 mg
Fiber: 2 g
Calcium: 41 mg

To balance your meal, add: Your choice of 5-Way Fish Fillet,
apple wedges*

Dilled Green Beans

Use this quick and easy recipe for a cold vegetable or a salad. It's particularly convenient for buffets because you won't have to worry about keeping it warm.

1 (9-ounce) package frozen French-cut green beans
¼ cup fat-free sour cream
¼ cup light mayonnaise
1 teaspoon dill weed
2 tablespoons cider vinegar
¼ cup green onion, chopped
½ teaspoon salt
2 tablespoons pimento, chopped (optional)

Blanch the beans for 1 minute. Drain them. Combine all of the ingredients. Refrigerate the beans until they're cold.

Makes 4 servings.

Calories per serving: 92
Protein: 2 g
Carbohydrates: 10 g
Fat: 5 g
Cholesterol: 6 mg
Fiber: 2 g
Calcium: 57 mg

To balance your meal, add: Flounder Parmesan,
melon wedge*

Oriental Spinach

This is a delightful change of flavor for spinach and a great
accompaniment for pork, chicken, beef, or lamb.

10 ounces fresh spinach leaves, torn into pieces
8 ounces water chestnuts, chopped
3 tablespoons green onion, chopped
1 tablespoon vegetable oil
¼ cup sweet and sour sauce
1 tablespoon soy sauce

Put the spinach in a 2-quart microwavable casserole dish. Add the
water chestnuts and onion. Microwave the vegetables on high for
3 to 4 minutes or until the spinach wilts. Stir and cover it, and set
it aside.

Put the oil and the sauces into a 1-cup glass measure. Microwave them on high for 1 minute. Pour the sauce over the spinach.
Toss it to serve.

Makes 4 servings.

Calories per serving: 95
Protein: 2 g
Carbohydrates: 14 g
Fat: 4 g
Cholesterol: 0
Fiber: 4 g
Calcium: 44 mg

To balance your meal, add: French Bread Pizza*,
orange wedges

Vegetable Pasta Primavera

This pasta recipe is light enough for a meatless meal or fun for a side dish. Cooking can't get much easier than this.

> 1 cup shell-shaped pasta or other small-shaped pasta, uncooked
> 1 teaspoon oil
> 2½ cups fresh vegetables (broccoli, green onions, red pepper, carrots), chopped
> ¼ cup Parmesan cheese, grated

Prepare the pasta according to the package directions. Drain it.

Heat the oil in a large skillet. Add the vegetables and stir-fry until they're tender-crisp. Add the pasta. Sprinkle it with the Parmesan cheese. Serve it immediately.

Makes 4 servings.

Calories per serving: 166
Protein: 7 g
Carbohydrates: 27 g
Fat: 4 g
Cholesterol: 5 mg
Fiber: 3 g
Calcium: 108 mg

To balance your meal, add: Sweet and Sour Glazed Chicken*

Upside-Down Biscuits

Fun, tasty, and a welcomed addition to any meal.

cooking spray
1 (10 ounce) can crushed pineapple
½ cup light brown sugar, packed
¼ cup margarine or butter, room temperature
5 maraschino cherries, cut in half
1 (12-ounce) can refrigerated buttermilk biscuits

Preheat the oven to 350 degrees F. Spray a muffin pan with the cooking spray. Drain the pineapple, reserving the juice.

In a large bowl, combine the pineapple, brown sugar, and margarine or butter. Mix them well. Divide the pineapple mixture among 10 cups in the muffin pan. Place a cherry half in the center of each, making sure the cherry hits the bottom of the cup.

Place 1 biscuit in each cup on top of the pineapple mixture. Spoon 1 teaspoon of the pineapple juice over each biscuit. Bake them for 8 to 10 minutes or as indicated on the biscuit can. Cool them at least 2 minutes. Invert the biscuits onto a warm plate to serve.

Makes 10 biscuits.

Calories per serving: 178
Protein: 3 g
Carbohydrates: 31 g
Fat: 5 g
Cholesterol: 5 mg
Fiber: 0
Calcium: 15 mg

To balance your meal, add: My Own Chicken Soup*,
fresh fruit cup

Southwestern Corn Salad

*Make a batch for tonight, and save some for a potluck
meal later in the week.*

1 (15-ounce) can black beans or black-eyed peas, rinsed
    and drained
1 (11-ounce) can Mexican-style yellow corn, drained
1 cup red onion or sweet white onion, finely chopped
¼ cup cilantro, chopped
¼ cup extra-virgin olive oil or vegetable oil
¼ cup lime juice
1 teaspoon jalapeno or serrano pepper, seeded, finely
    chopped
lettuce leaves

Combine the black beans or black-eyed peas, corn, onion,
cilantro, oil, lime juice, and pepper in a bowl. Cover and refrigerate this for at least 1 hour to blend the flavors. Serve the corn
salad over the lettuce.

Makes 6 servings.

Calories per serving: 165
Protein: 4 g
Carbohydrates: 21 g
Fat: 9 g
Cholesterol: 0
Fiber: 5 g
Calcium: 32 mg

To balance your meal, add: Quick Tamale Casserole*

Spinach and Wild Rice

Adding spinach to classic rice infuses it with flavor,
color, and nutrients.

1 (6-ounce) box long grain and wild rice
1 (10-ounce) bag fresh spinach
1 tablespoon butter
2 tablespoons Parmesan cheese, grated

Prepare the rice according to the package directions.

Place the spinach and butter in a microwavable bowl. Cover and cook it for about 1 minute. Stir the rice mixture into the spinach; microwave it for approximately 3 more minutes. Let it stand for 2 minutes. Sprinkle it with the Parmesan cheese to serve.

Makes 6 servings.

Calories per serving: 132
Protein: 4 g
Carbohydrates: 23 g
Fat: 3 g
Cholesterol: 4 mg
Fiber: 1 g
Calcium: 88 mg

To balance your meal, add: Southwestern Salmon*

Broccoli Rice

*To reduce the fat, you can substitute fat-free mushroom
soup for the regular soup.*

1 tablespoon vegetable oil
1 medium onion, chopped
2 cups rice, cooked
1 (10-ounce) package chopped frozen broccoli, cooked
1 (10¾-ounce) can cream of mushroom soup
1 (8-ounce) jar processed cheese sauce

Preheat the oven to 350 degrees F.

In a large skillet, heat the oil. Add the onion and cook it until
the onion is tender. Add the cooked rice, broccoli, soup, and
cheese sauce to the skillet. Mix them well.

Pour the mixture into a 2-quart casserole dish and bake it for
15 minutes.

Makes 8 servings.

Calories per serving: 210
Protein: 6 g
Carbohydrates: 22 g
Fat: 11 g
Cholesterol: 22 mg
Fiber: 2 g
Calcium: 135 mg

To balance your meal, add: Steak and Veggies in Foil*

Zucchini Cornbread Squares

These squares make an excellent snack item for a sack lunch or even work well as an appetizer to a meal.

cooking spray
4 eggs
1 (8½-ounce) box cornbread mix
½ cup onion, chopped
½ teaspoon Tabasco sauce (optional)
1 cup low-fat cheddar cheese, shredded
3 medium zucchini squash, coarsely grated
    (approximately 4 cups)

Preheat the oven to 350 degrees F. Spray a 9-by-13-inch pan with the cooking spray.

Beat the eggs. Add the cornbread mix, onion, Tabasco, and cheese. Add the grated zucchini to the cornbread mixture. Pour the batter into the prepared pan. Bake the cornbread for 25 to 30 minutes until it's golden brown. Serve immediately.

Makes 12 servings.

Calories per serving: 131
Protein: 6 g
Carbohydrates: 16 g
Fat: 5 g
Cholesterol: 65 mg
Fiber: 2 g
Calcium: 66 mg

To balance your meal, add: Quick and Easy Vegetable Stir Fry*, Angel Food Cake with Strawberries*

SNACKS

Spinach Dip

Serve your dip in a hollowed-out bread bowl for added fun.

- 1 (10-ounce) package frozen spinach, thawed and drained well
- 1 (8-ounce) container fat-free or low-fat sour cream
- ⅓ cup light mayonnaise
- ½ (1⅖-ounce) package dry vegetable soup mix
- 1 (8-ounce) can water chestnuts, finely chopped
- 1 stalk celery, finely chopped

In a large bowl, combine the drained spinach with the remaining ingredients. Cover and chill these before serving. Serve the dip with fresh vegetables, bread chunks, or crackers.

Makes about 4 cups, about 2 tablespoons per serving.

Calories per serving: 27
Protein: 1 g
Carbohydrates: 4 g
Fat: 1 g
Cholesterol: 1 mg
Fiber: 1 g
Calcium: 24 mg

Mexican Bean Dip

Full of beans, this dip is high in fiber and in taste. Serve with tortilla chips or pita bread.

1½ cups kidney, pinto, or black beans, cooked or canned, drained
¼ cup tomato paste
2 teaspoons red wine vinegar
2 teaspoons chili powder
½ teaspoon ground cumin
¼ teaspoon garlic powder
2 tablespoons green onion, chopped

Puree the beans in a blender or a food processor until they're smooth. Transfer them to a medium bowl and add the remaining ingredients. Mix everything well.

Makes 8 servings.

Calories per serving: 67
Protein: 4 g
Carbohydrates: 12 g
Fat: 0
Cholesterol: 0
Fiber: 5 g
Calcium: 6 mg

Hot Salmon Dip

Shape this into a ball and serve it cold, if preferred, rather than baking it and serving it hot. Whatever your mood!

1 (7¾-ounce) can boneless salmon, drained
1 (8-ounce) package light cream cheese, softened
2 tablespoons onion, chopped
1 tablespoon low-fat milk
¾ teaspoon horseradish
¼ teaspoon dill weed
¼ teaspoon black pepper
½ cup almonds, slivered

Preheat the oven to 375 degrees F. In a medium bowl, combine all of the ingredients except the almonds. Mix them well. Spoon the mixture into an oven-proof dish. Sprinkle half of the almonds on top of the mixture. Bake it for 10 minutes. Sprinkle the remaining almonds on top. Serve with fresh vegetables, crackers, bagel chips, or pita chips.

Makes 16 servings, about 1 tablespoon per serving.

Calories per serving: 42
Protein: 4 g
Carbohydrates: 1 g
Fat: 2 g
Cholesterol: 11 mg
Fiber: 0
Calcium: 45 mg

Italian Bread Knots

These are easy to make and a fun project for kids, too.

> 2 tablespoons Parmesan cheese, grated
> ½ teaspoon Italian seasoning
> 1 (11-ounce) can breadstick dough

Preheat the oven to 400 degrees F.

On a small plate, combine the Parmesan cheese and Italian seasoning. Separate the breadsticks from the can and roll each one in the cheese mixture. Twist and fold each one to form a knot shape. Place them on a baking sheet.

Bake them for 15 minutes or until they're golden brown. Serve them hot or use them as a side in a packed lunch.

Makes 12 bread knots, 1 per serving.

Calories per serving: 78
Protein: 2 g
Carbohydrates: 13 g
Fat: 2 g
Cholesterol: 1 mg
Fiber: 0
Calcium: 14 mg

Oatmeal Cookie Sandwiches

Keep these handy in the freezer for a quick treat.

4 oatmeal cookies
¼ cup low-fat vanilla frozen yogurt

Lay 2 cookies bottom-side up. Spread half of the frozen yogurt onto each cookie. Top it with the remaining cookie. Wrap the sandwiches in plastic wrap and freeze them until you're ready to eat them.

Makes 2 sandwiches.

Calories per serving: 153
Protein: 3 g
Carbohydrates: 23 g
Fat: 6 g
Cholesterol: 1 mg
Fiber: 1 g
Calcium: 41 mg

Carrot Applesauce Cupcakes with Lemon Cream Cheese Frosting

For variety, make these in a mini-cupcake pan for a smaller snack size or a lunch box treat.

cooking spray
1 cup flour
⅓ cup sugar
1½ teaspoons baking powder
¼ teaspoon baking soda
¼ teaspoon salt
½ cup unsweetened applesauce
1 egg
¼ cup oil
¾ cups carrots, grated

Topping:
2 ounces cream cheese, softened
½ teaspoon lemon juice
½–1 cup confectioner's sugar

Preheat the oven to 350 degrees F. Spray a muffin pan with the cooking spray.

In a large bowl, combine the flour, sugar, baking powder, baking soda, and salt.

In another bowl, combine the applesauce, egg, and oil. Stir in the carrots. Fold the liquid ingredients into the dry ingredients and combine until they're just moistened. Pour the batter into the muffin pan cups to two-thirds full. Bake the cupcakes for 30 minutes or until a toothpick inserted comes out clean. Remove the cupcakes from the oven. Cool them.

Beat the frosting ingredients until the mixture is smooth. Spread it over the cooled cupcakes.

Makes 1 dozen cupcakes.

Calories per serving: 145
Protein: 2 g
Carbohydrates: 20 g
Fat: 7 g
Cholesterol: 21 mg
Fiber: 1 g
Calcium: 43 mg

Carrot Oatmeal Raisin Cookies

The kids will love these, and Mom will appreciate that her kids enjoy eating such nutritious cookies. Also, try adding dried cherries or cranberries in place of the raisins for a change.

1 egg
½ cup vegetable oil
½ cup sugar
½ cup brown sugar
1 cup flour
¼ teaspoon baking soda
¼ teaspoon salt
½ teaspoon ground cinnamon
1¼ cups rolled oats
1 cup carrots, finely grated
¼ cup raisins

Preheat the oven to 350 degrees F. In a large bowl, combine the egg, oil, and sugars. Mix them well.

In a medium bowl, combine the flour, baking soda, salt, and cinnamon. Stir the flour mixture into the egg mixture. Add the oats, carrots, and raisins.

Drop the cookie dough by tablespoonfuls onto an ungreased cookie sheet, placing them 2 inches apart. Bake the cookies 12 minutes or until they're golden brown.

Makes 2 dozen cookies (1 cookie per serving).

Calories per serving: 118
Protein: 1 g
Carbohydrates: 17 g
Fat: 5 g
Cholesterol: 8 mg
Fiber: 1 g
Calcium: 10 mg

Apple Cinnamon Crisp

For a new and different taste, add raisins, dried cranberries, or almonds to the crumb mixture.

cooking spray
4 apples, peeled and sliced
1 cup rolled oats
½ cup brown sugar
¼ cup flour
1 teaspoon ground cinnamon
½ teaspoon ground nutmeg
3 tablespoons margarine or butter, melted

Preheat the oven to 350 degrees F. Spray a 9-inch pie pan with the cooking spray. Lay the apple slices over the bottom of the prepared pan.

In a medium bowl, combine the oats, brown sugar, flour, cinnamon, and nutmeg. Add the melted margarine or butter and mix well.

Spread the crumb mixture over the top of the apple slices. Bake the crisp 45 minutes or until it's golden brown on top.

Makes 8 servings.

Calories per serving: 185
Protein: 2 g
Carbohydrates: 34 g
Fat: 5 g
Cholesterol: 5 mg
Fiber: 3 g
Calcium: 27 mg

Popcorn Peanut Butter Delights

Kids' favorites are combined in one recipe—
what a great treat for all!

½ cup creamy peanut butter
½ cup margarine or butter
1 (10½-ounce) package miniature marshmallows
6 cups popcorn, freshly popped
6 cups spoon-sized shredded wheat
1 cup peanuts, dry roasted
1 cup raisins

Preheat the oven to 250 degrees F. Place paper liners in two 12-cup muffin pans.

Melt the peanut butter and margarine or butter in a large microwavable bowl on high for 1 minute. Add the marshmallows. Heat it for another minute or until the marshmallows puff; stir.

Add the popcorn, shredded wheat, peanuts, and raisins; stir gently. Divide the mixture into 24 cups. Bake the delights for 10 minutes. Cool and store them in airtight containers.

Makes 24 delights, 1 per serving.

Calories per serving: 207
Protein: 5 g
Carbohydrates: 28 g
Fat: 10 g
Cholesterol: 4 mg
Fiber: 3 g
Calcium: 13 mg

Fresh Fruit Pizza

Add different types of fruit that your family enjoys.

cooking spray
1 (8-ounce) package refrigerated sugar cookie dough
1 (8-ounce) container nondairy whipped topping, thawed
1 cup strawberries, sliced
1 cup pineapple chunks
½ cup blueberries
½ cup raspberries

Spray a 16-inch round flat pizza pan with the cooking spray. Spread the cookie dough over the bottom of the pizza pan. Bake it according to the package directions. Let it cool.

Spread the whipped topping over the top of the cooled dough. Top it with the assorted fruit slices and berries. Refrigerate the pizza until you're ready to serve it.

Makes 12 servings.

Calories per serving: 161
Protein: 1 g
Carbohydrates: 20 g
Fat: 9 g
Cholesterol: 6 mg
Fiber: 1 g
Calcium: 22 mg

Raspberry Coffee Cake

*This cake is similar in texture to a sour cream
coffee cake but is made with low-fat yogurt.
It is moist, delicious, and appealing.*

cooking spray
2 cups flour
1 teaspoon baking powder
¾ teaspoon baking soda
¼ teaspoon ground cinnamon
¼ teaspoon ground nutmeg
1¼ cups fresh raspberries
½ cup margarine or butter
½ cup sugar
2 eggs
¼ cup plain low-fat yogurt
2 teaspoons vanilla extract
Topping:
2 teaspoons margarine or butter
2 tablespoons pecans, chopped
1 tablespoon sugar
½ teaspoon ground cinnamon

Preheat the oven to 350 degrees F. Spray an 8-by-8-inch pan with
the cooking spray.

In a medium bowl, combine the flour, baking powder, baking
soda, cinnamon, and nutmeg. In a separate small bowl, toss the
raspberries with 1 tablespoon of the flour mixture. Set them
aside.

In a mixing bowl, cream the margarine or butter and sugar.
Add the eggs and blend well. Add the flour mixture. Stir in the
yogurt and vanilla. Fold in the raspberries. Pour the mixture into
the prepared pan.

Combine the topping ingredients. Sprinkle them over the batter. Bake the cake for 45 minutes or until it is done. Cool it before serving.

Makes 12 servings.

Calories per serving: 219
Protein: 4 g
Carbohydrates: 28 g
Fat: 10 g
Cholesterol: 45 mg
Fiber: 2 g
Calcium: 48 mg

Creamy Coconut Cake

Add some color and garnish your cake with fresh raspberries, strawberries, blueberries, or all three.

1 (18½-ounce) package yellow cake mix
1½ cups low-fat milk
½ cup sugar
2 cups flaked coconut, divided
1 (8-ounce) carton nondairy whipped topping, thawed

Prepare the cake mix as directed on the package, baked in a 9-by-13-inch pan. Cool it for 15 minutes. Poke holes all over the top of the cooled cake with a fork.

In a medium saucepan, combine the milk, sugar, and ½ cup of the coconut. Bring this to a boil; reduce the heat and simmer it 1 minute. Carefully spoon all the liquid over the cake, allowing the liquid to soak down through the holes. Cool the cake completely.

Fold ½ cup of the coconut into the whipped topping and spread it over the top of the cake. Sprinkle it with the remaining coconut. Chill the cake overnight and serve it cut into squares.

Makes 24 servings.

Calories per serving: 168
Protein: 2 g
Carbohydrates: 28 g
Fat: 6 g
Cholesterol: 1 mg
Fiber: 1 g
Calcium: 52 mg

Spicy Popcorn and Peanuts

Make a batch for TV night or a friendly football game.

3 tablespoons margarine or butter
2 teaspoons chili powder
1 cup peanuts, roasted
10 cups popcorn, popped

In a small skillet, melt the margarine or butter. Add the chili powder. Mix together well. Cool slightly.

In a large bowl combine the peanuts and popcorn. Toss them well with the chili powder mixture.

Makes 12 servings.

Calories per serving: 123
Protein: 4 g
Carbohydrates: 8 g
Fat: 9 g
Cholesterol: 3 mg
Fiber: 2 g
Calcium: 9 mg

Summer Dessert

You will find these fruits more available in the summer.
You'll love putting together this refreshing dessert.
It's a great ending to a barbecue.

1 cup fresh seedless grapes, halved
1 cup fresh whole blueberries
1 cup fresh peaches, cut into bite-size pieces
1 cup fresh strawberries, halved
½ cup light brown sugar, firmly packed
1 cup light sour cream

Wash and cut the fruit. In a large bowl, combine all of the fruit. Pour it into a shallow 9-by-2-inch glass dish. Sprinkle the brown sugar over the fruit. Top it with the sour cream and cover it with plastic wrap. Refrigerate it for 3 to 4 hours. (The sour cream will seep through the brown sugar to the fruit.)

To serve, gently stir the fruit and spoon it into fruit bowls or sherbet glasses.

Makes 8 servings.

Calories per serving: 138
Protein: 2 g
Carbohydrates: 25 g
Fat: 4 g
Cholesterol: 15 mg
Fiber: 2 g
Calcium: 69 mg

Fruit Sorbet

Making your own fruit sorbet can be a fun family project.

1 (20-ounce) package frozen mixed fruit (peaches, melon,
    strawberries, grapes)
½ cup apple juice
½ cup carbonated soda water
¼ cup sugar

Using a food processor, pulse the fruit 15 to 20 times until it is
chunky. Add the juice, soda water, and sugar. Process it 1 to 2
minutes until it's smooth. Chill it in the freezer until it's ready to
serve.

Makes 4 servings.

Calories per serving: 201
Protein: 2 g
Carbohydrates: 50 g
Fat: 0
Cholesterol: 0
Fiber: 3 g
Calcium: 14 mg

Angel Food Cake with Strawberries

Let your kids prepare this simple, tasty dessert.

1 (8-ounce) package fresh strawberries
½ cup strawberry syrup
1 prepared angel food cake
4 ounces nondairy whipped topping

Rinse the strawberries and remove the stems. Slice the berries and place them in a small bowl. Add the strawberry syrup and stir it to coat the berries.

Slice the cake into 12 portions. Place a slice of cake onto a serving plate. Top it with the strawberry mixture and whipped topping, as desired. Serve immediately.

Makes 12 servings.

Calories per serving: 164
Protein: 3 g
Carbohydrates: 37 g
Fat: 1 g
Cholesterol: 0
Fiber: 1 g
Calcium: 66 mg

Old Fashioned Bread Pudding

Here's a great way to use up leftover bread.

cooking spray
3 cups day-old (or older) French bread, cut into cubes,
   about 6 slices
3 cups low-fat milk
¾ cup sugar
3 eggs, slightly beaten
½ teaspoon salt
1 teaspoon vanilla extract

Preheat the oven to 350 degrees F. Spray a 9-by-9-inch baking pan with the cooking spray. Place the bread cubes in the pan.

Whisk together the milk, sugar, eggs, salt, and vanilla. Pour this over the bread cubes. Place the baking dish in a larger pan of water to keep the custard from cooking too fast.

Bake the pudding for 45 to 60 minutes, until a knife inserted in the middle of the pan comes out clean.

Serve it warm or cold. Fruit toppings can be added for color and a different taste.

Makes 8 servings.

Calories per serving: 195
Protein: 7 g
Carbohydrates: 33 g
Fat: 4 g
Cholesterol: 77 mg
Fiber: 0
Calcium: 134 mg

Resources

Dietary Guidelines for Americans, 2005
Outline and advice to promote health and to reduce risk for major chronic
diseases through diet and physical activity
www.health.gov/dietaryguidelines/dga2005/document/

Centers for Disease Control and Prevention for Everyone
Resources on health and physical activity for various age groups
www.cdc.gov

U.S. Food and Drug Administration, Center for Food Safety and Applied Nutrition
Guidance on nutrition labeling and home food safety
www.cfsan.fda.gov/

MyPyramid
Created by the USDA; assists individuals in choosing the foods and the
amounts that are right for them
www.mypyramid.gov/guidelines

Healthy People, 2010
Challenges individuals, communities, and professionals to take specific
steps to ensure that good health, as well as long life, are enjoyed by all
www.healthypeople.gov

American Dietetic Association
Your source for adequate information on nutrition and health—the official
site of the American Dietetic Association, with nearly 65,000 members.
Includes Nationwide Nutrition Network, a national referral service that
links consumers, physicians, food manufacturers and distributors, and
restaurant owners and managers with dietetic professionals
www.eatright.org

American Heart Association
Healthful advice and information from the American Heart Association on
being heart healthy, eating heart healthy, and understanding the risks of
heart disease
www.americanheart.org

National Dairy Council
Guidance on the importance of dairy foods in the diet for children and adults
www.nationaldairycouncil.org

Index

About the Authors

Sandra K. Nissenberg, M.S., R.D., is a registered dietitian and currently works full time as a cookbook editor. Sandra, the author of twelve books on nutrition, primarily in the area of child nutrition, has written books to help busy families like her own. She is the mother of two active teenagers and continues to focus on helping working parents find solutions to feeding their children healthfully while maintaining a career. Sandra, her husband, and her children live in Buffalo Grove, Illinois.

Margaret L. Bogle, Ph.D., R.D., is the executive director of the Lower Mississippi Delta Nutrition Intervention Research Initiative and is employed by the Agricultural Research Service of the United States Department of Agriculture. She has spent most of her career as a pediatric nutritionist working extensively with families and children. She has served on the board of directors of the American Dietetic Association and its foundation.

Audrey C. Wright, M.S., is the former director of Father Walter Memorial Child Care Center in Montgomery, Alabama, where she continues to serve on its Advisory Board of Directors. Audrey is active in the American Dietetic Association and has served on the board of directors of both the association and its foundation.